Committee on National Security Systems

CNSS Instruction No. 4009
26 April 2010

National

Information Assurance (IA)

Glossary

This document prescribes minimum standards.
Your department or agency may require further implementation guidelines.

National Manager

FOREWORD

1. The Committee on National Security Systems (CNSS) Glossary Working Group convened to review and update the National Information Assurance Glossary, CNSSI 4009, dated June 2006. This revision of CNSSI 4009 incorporates many new terms submitted by the CNSS Membership. Most of the terms from the 2006 version of the Glossary remain, but a number of them have updated definitions in order to remove inconsistencies among the communities.

2. The Glossary Working Group set several overall objectives for itself in producing this version:

- Resolve differences between the definitions of terms used by the DOD, IC, and Civil Agencies (NIST Glossary) to enable all three to use the same glossary (and move towards shared documentation and processes).
- Accommodate the transition from Certification and Accreditation (C&A) terms in current use to the terms now appearing in documents produced by the C&A Transformation initiative. Both sets of terms have been included in this update of the glossary.
- Ensure consistency among related and dependent terms.
- Include terms that are important to the risk management goal of C&A transformation and to the concept of information sharing.
- Review existing definitions to reflect, as appropriate a broader *enterprise* perspective vice a *system* perspective.
- Strike an appropriate balance between macro terms and micro terms (i.e., include terms that are useful in writing and understanding documents dealing with IA policies, directives, instructions, and guidance, and strike terms that are useful only to specific IA subspecialties).

3. Many cyber terms are coming into vogue and the Glossary Working Group has tried to include significant examples that have a useful distinction when compared to existing Information Assurance terms. A number of terms recommended for inclusion in this version of the glossary were not added – often because they appeared to have a narrow application or they were submitted after the deadline. But the net affect has been to add quite a few new terms to the glossary.

4. When glossary terms have common acronyms, we have noted the acronym with the term and added the acronym to the acronym list. In some instances, there may be several meanings for the same acronym, and in that case we have tried to list all the common IA meanings. Note that some acronyms are self-explanatory, and so there is no definition of these acronyms in the glossary itself.

5. Some terms from the previous version were deleted because they had been previously marked as candidates for deletion (C.F.D.) and no one asked to keep them, many other terms have been updated or added, and some terms are newly identified as C.F.D. If a term that has been deleted or marked as C.F.D. is still of value and needed in your environment, please resubmit the term with a definition based on the following criteria: 1) specific relevance to Information Assurance; 2) economy of words; 3)

accuracy; 4) broad applicability; and 5) clarity. Use these same criteria to recommend any changes to existing definitions or to suggest new terms (definitions must be included with any new terms). When recommending a change to an existing definition, please note how that change might affect other terms. In all cases, send your suggestions to the CNSS Secretariat via e-mail or fax at the number found below.

6. We recognize that, to remain useful, a glossary must be in a continuous state of coordination, and we encourage your review and welcome your comments as new terms become significant and old terms fall into disuse or change meaning. The goal of the Glossary Working Group is to keep the Glossary relevant and a tool for commonality among the IA community.

7. Representatives of the CNSS may obtain copies of this instruction on the CNSS Web Page www.cnss.gov.

FOR THE NATIONAL MANAGER:

/s/
RICHARD C. SCHAEFFER, JR.

NATIONAL INFORMATION ASSURANCE (IA) GLOSSARY

This instruction applies to all U.S. Government Departments, Agencies, Bureaus and Offices; supporting contractors and agents; that collect, generate process, store, display, transmit or receive classified or sensitive information or that operate, use, or connect to National Security Systems (NSS), as defined herein.

A

access	Ability and means to communicate with or otherwise interact with a system, to use system resources to handle information, to gain knowledge of the information the system contains, or to control system components and functions.
access authority	An entity responsible for monitoring and granting access privileges for other authorized entities.
access control	The process of granting or denying specific requests: 1) for obtaining and using information and related information processing services; and 2) to enter specific physical facilities (e.g., Federal buildings, military establishments, and border crossing entrances).
Access Control List (ACL)	1. A list of permissions associated with an object. The list specifies who or what is allowed to access the object and what operations are allowed to be performed on the object. 2. A mechanism that implements access control for a system resource by enumerating the system entities that are permitted to access the resource and stating, either implicitly or explicitly, the access modes granted to each entity.
access control mechanism	Security safeguards (i.e., hardware and software features, physical controls, operating procedures, management procedures, and various combinations of these) designed to detect and deny unauthorized access and permit authorized access to an information system.
access level	A category within a given security classification limiting entry or system connectivity to only authorized persons.
access list	Roster of individuals authorized admittance to a controlled area.
access profile	Association of a user with a list of protected objects the user may access.

access type	Privilege to perform action on an object. Read, write, execute, append, modify, delete, and create are examples of access types. See write.
accountability	Principle that an individual is entrusted to safeguard and control equipment, keying material, and information and is answerable to proper authority for the loss or misuse of that equipment or information.
Accounting Legend Code (ALC)	Numeric code used to indicate the minimum accounting controls required for items of accountable COMSEC material within the COMSEC Material Control System.
accounting number	Number assigned to an item of COMSEC material to facilitate its control.
accreditation	Formal declaration by a Designated Accrediting Authority (DAA) or Principal Accrediting Authority (PAA) that an information system is approved to operate at an acceptable level of risk, based on the implementation of an approved set of technical, managerial, and procedural safeguards. See authorization.
accreditation boundary	1. Identifies the information resources covered by an accreditation decision, as distinguished from separately accredited information resources that are interconnected or with which information is exchanged via messaging. Synonymous with Security Perimeter. 2. For the purposes of identifying the Protection Level for confidentiality of a system to be accredited, the system has a conceptual boundary that extends to all intended users of the system, both directly and indirectly connected, who receive output from the system. See authorization boundary.
accreditation package	Product comprised of a System Security Plan (SSP) and a report documenting the basis for the accreditation decision.
Accrediting Authority	Synonymous with Designated Accrediting Authority (DAA). See also Authorizing Official.
active attack	An attack that alters a system or data.
active content	Software in various forms that is able to automatically carry out or trigger actions on a computer platform without the intervention of a user.
add-on security	Incorporation of new or additional hardware, software, or firmware safeguards in an operational information system.
adequate security	Security commensurate with the risk and magnitude of harm resulting from the loss, misuse, or unauthorized access to or modification of information. Note: This includes assuring that information systems operate effectively and provide appropriate confidentiality, integrity, and availability, through the use of cost-effective management, personnel, operational, and technical controls.

Advanced Encryption Standard (AES)	A U.S. Government-approved cryptographic algorithm that can be used to protect electronic data. The AES algorithm is a symmetric block cipher that can encrypt (encipher) and decrypt (decipher) information.
Advanced Key Processor (AKP)	A cryptographic device that performs all cryptographic functions for a management client node and contains the interfaces to 1) exchange information with a client platform, 2) interact with fill devices, and 3) connect a client platform securely to the primary services node (PRSN).
advisory	Notification of significant new trends or developments regarding the threat to the information systems of an organization. This notification may include analytical insights into trends, intentions, technologies, or tactics of an adversary targeting information systems.
alert	Notification that a specific attack has been directed at an organization's information systems.
alternate COMSEC custodian	Individual designated by proper authority to perform the duties of the COMSEC custodian during the temporary absence of the COMSEC custodian.
anti-jam	Countermeasures ensuring that transmitted information can be received despite deliberate jamming attempts.
anti-spoof	Countermeasures taken to prevent the unauthorized use of legitimate Identification & Authentication (I&A) data, however it was obtained, to mimic a subject different from the attacker.
application	Software program that performs a specific function directly for a user and can be executed without access to system control, monitoring, or administrative privileges.
Approval to Operate (ATO)	The official management decision issued by a DAA or PAA to authorize operation of an information system and to explicitly accept the residual risk to agency operations (including mission, functions, image, or reputation), agency assets, or individuals. See authorization to operate.
asset	A major application, general support system, high impact program, physical plant, mission critical system, personnel, equipment, or a logically related group of systems.
assurance	Measure of confidence that the security features, practices, procedures, and architecture of an information system accurately mediates and enforces the security policy.
assured information sharing	The ability to confidently share information with those who need it, when and where they need it, as determined by operational need and an acceptable level of security risk.
assured software	Computer application that has been designed, developed, analyzed and tested using processes, tools, and techniques that establish a level of confidence in it.

asymmetric cryptography	See public key cryptography.
attack	Any kind of malicious activity that attempts to collect, disrupt, deny, degrade, or destroy information system resources or the information itself.
Attack Sensing and Warning (AS&W)	Detection, correlation, identification, and characterization of intentional unauthorized activity with notification to decision makers so that an appropriate response can be developed.
attack signature	A characteristic byte pattern used in malicious code or an indicator, or set of indicators that allows the identification of malicious network activities.
attribute-based access control	Access control based on attributes associated with and about subjects, objects, targets, initiators, resources, or the environment. An access control rule set defines the combination of attributes under which an access may take place.
attribute-based authorization	A structured process that determines when a user is authorized to access information, systems, or services based on attributes of the user and of the information, system, or service.
audit	Independent review and examination of records and activities to assess the adequacy of system controls and ensure compliance with established policies and operational procedures.
audit log	A chronological record of system activities. Includes records of system accesses and operations performed in a given period.
audit reduction tools	Preprocessors designed to reduce the volume of audit records to facilitate manual review. Before a security review, these tools can remove many audit records known to have little security significance. These tools generally remove records generated by specified classes of events, such as records generated by nightly backups.
audit trail	A chronological record that reconstructs and examines the sequence of activities surrounding or leading to a specific operation, procedure, or event in a security relevant transaction from inception to final result.
authenticate	To verify the identity of a user, user device, or other entity.
authentication	The process of verifying the identity or other attributes claimed by or assumed of an entity (user, process, or device), or to verify the source and integrity of data.
	NIST SP 800-53: Verifying the identity of a user, process, or device, often as a prerequisite to allowing access to resources in an information system.
authentication mechanism	Hardware or software-based algorithm that forces users, devices, or processes to prove their identity before accessing data on an information system.

authentication period	The maximum acceptable period between any initial authentication process and subsequent re-authentication processes during a single terminal session or during the period data is being accessed.
authentication protocol	A well specified message exchange process between a claimant and a verifier that enables the verifier to confirm the claimant's identity.
authenticator	The means used to confirm the identity of a user, process, or device (e.g., user password or token).
authenticity	The property of being genuine and being able to be verified and trusted; confidence in the validity of a transmission, a message, or message originator. See Authentication.
authority	Person(s) or established bodies with rights and responsibilities to exert control in an administrative sphere.
authorization	Access privileges granted to a user, program, or process or the act of granting those privileges.
authorization (to operate)	The official management decision given by a senior organizational official to authorize operation of an information system and to explicitly accept the risk to organizational operations (including mission, functions, image, or reputation), organizational assets, individuals, other organizations, and the Nation based on the implementation of an agreed-upon set of security controls.
authorization boundary	All components of an information system to be authorized for operation by an authorizing official and excludes separately authorized systems, to which the information system is connected.
authorized vendor	Manufacturer of information assurance equipment authorized to produce quantities in excess of contractual requirements for direct sale to eligible buyers. Eligible buyers are typically U.S. Government organizations or U.S. Government contractors.
Authorized Vendor Program (AVP) (C.F.D.)	Program in which a vendor, producing an INFOSEC product under contract to NSA, is authorized to produce that product in numbers exceeding the contracted requirements for direct marketing and sale to eligible buyers. Eligible buyers are typically U.S. Government organizations or U.S. Government contractors. Products approved for marketing and sale through the AVP are placed on the Endorsed Cryptographic Products List (ECPL).
Authorizing Official	Senior (federal) official or executive with the authority to formally assume responsibility for operating an information system at an acceptable level of risk to organizational operations (including mission, functions, image, or reputation), organizational assets, individuals, other organizations, and the Nation.

Authorizing Official Designated Representative	An organizational official acting on behalf of an authorizing official in carrying out and coordinating the required activities associated with security authorization.
automated security monitoring	Use of automated procedures to ensure security controls are not circumvented or the use of these tools to track actions taken by subjects suspected of misusing the information system.
automatic remote rekeying	Procedure to rekey distant cryptographic equipment electronically without specific actions by the receiving terminal operator. See manual remote rekeying.
availability	The property of being accessible and useable upon demand by an authorized entity. NIST 800-53: Ensuring timely and reliable access to and use of information.

B

back door	Typically unauthorized hidden software or hardware mechanism used to circumvent security controls.
backup	Copy of files and programs made to facilitate recovery, if necessary.
banner	Display on an information system that sets parameters for system or data use.
baseline	Hardware, software, databases, and relevant documentation for an information system at a given point in time.
bastion host	A special purpose computer on a network specifically designed and configured to withstand attacks.
benign environment	A non-hostile location protected from external hostile elements by physical, personnel, and procedural security countermeasures.
binding	Process of associating two or more related elements of information.
biometrics	Measurable physical characteristics or personal behavioral traits used to identify, or verify the claimed identity, of an individual. Facial images, fingerprints, and handwriting samples are all examples of biometrics.
bit	A contraction of the term Binary Digit. The smallest unit of information in a binary system of notation.
bit error rate	Ratio between the number of bits incorrectly received and the total number of bits transmitted in a telecommunications system.
BLACK	Designation applied to encrypted information and the information systems, the associated areas, circuits, components, and equipment processing that information. See also RED.

black core	A communication network architecture in which user data traversing a global IP network is end-to-end encrypted at the IP layer. Related to striped core.
blacklisting	The process of the system invalidating a user ID based on the user's inappropriate actions. A blacklisted user ID cannot be used to log on to the system, even with the correct authenticator. Blacklisting and lifting of a blacklisting are both security-relevant events. Blacklisting also applies to blocks placed against IP addresses to prevent inappropriate or unauthorized use of internet resources.
blended attack	A hostile action to spread malicious code via multiple methods.
Blue Team	1. The group responsible for defending an enterprise's use of information systems by maintaining its security posture against a group of mock attackers (i.e., the Red Team). Typically the Blue Team and its supporters must defend against real or simulated attacks 1) over a significant period of time, 2) in a representative operational context (e.g., as part of an operational exercise), and 3) according to rules established and monitored with the help of a neutral group refereeing the simulation or exercise (i.e., the White Team).
	2. The term Blue Team is also used for defining a group of individuals that conduct operational network vulnerability evaluations and provide mitigation techniques to customers who have a need for an independent technical review of their network security posture. The Blue Team identifies security threats and risks in the operating environment, and in cooperation with the customer, analyzes the network environment and its current state of security readiness. Based on the Blue Team findings and expertise, they provide recommendations that integrate into an overall community security solution to increase the customer's cyber security readiness posture. Often times a Blue Team is employed by itself or prior to a Red Team employment to ensure that the customer's networks are as secure as possible before having the Red Team test the systems.
Body of Evidence (BoE)	The set of data that documents the information system's adherence to the security controls applied. The BoE will include a Requirements Verification Traceability Matrix (RVTM) delineating where the selected security controls are met and evidence to that fact can be found. The BoE content required by an Authorizing Official will be adjusted according to the impact levels selected.
boundary	Physical or logical perimeter of a system.
boundary protection	Monitoring and control of communications at the external boundary of an information system to prevent and detect malicious and other unauthorized communications, through the use of boundary protection devices (e.g., proxies, gateways, routers, firewalls, guards, encrypted tunnels).

boundary protection device	A device with appropriate mechanisms that facilitates the adjudication of different security policies for interconnected systems. NIST SP 800.53: A device with appropriate mechanisms that: (i) facilitates the adjudication of different interconnected system security policies (e.g., controlling the flow of information into or out of an interconnected system); and/or (ii) provides information system boundary protection.
browsing	Act of searching through information system storage or active content to locate or acquire information, without necessarily knowing the existence or format of information being sought.
buffer overflow	A condition at an interface under which more input can be placed into a buffer or data holding area than the capacity allocated, overwriting other information. Attackers exploit such a condition to crash a system or to insert specially crafted code that allows them to gain control of the system.
bulk encryption	Simultaneous encryption of all channels of a multi-channel telecommunications link.
Business Continuity Plan (BCP)	The documentation of a predetermined set of instructions or procedures that describe how an organization's business functions will be sustained during and after a significant disruption.
Business Impact Analysis (BIA)	An analysis of an enterprise's requirements, processes, and interdependencies used to characterize information system contingency requirements and priorities in the event of a significant disruption.

C

call back	Procedure for identifying and authenticating a remote information system terminal, whereby the host system disconnects the terminal and reestablishes contact.
canister	Type of protective package used to contain and dispense keying material in punched or printed tape form.
cascading (C.F.D.)	Downward flow of information through a range of security levels greater than the accreditation range of a system network or component.
category	Restrictive label applied to classified or unclassified information to limit access.
Central Office of Record (COR)	Office of a federal department or agency that keeps records of accountable COMSEC material held by elements subject to its oversight.
Central Services Node (CSN)	The Key Management Infrastructure core node that provides central security management and data management services.

certificate	A digitally signed representation of information that 1) identifies the authority issuing it, 2) identifies the subscriber, 3) identifies its valid operational period (date issued / expiration date). In the IA community certificate usually implies public key certificate and can have the following types:
	cross certificate – A certificate issued from a CA that signs the public key of another CA not within its trust hierarchy that establishes a trust relationship between the two CAs.
	encryption certificate – A certificate containing a public key that can encrypt or decrypt electronic messages, files, documents, or data transmissions, or establish or exchange a session key for these same purposes. Key management sometimes refers to the process of storing protecting and escrowing the private component of the key pair associated with the encryption certificate.
	identity certificate – A certificate that provides authentication of the identity claimed. Within the NSS PKI, identity certificates may be used only for authentication or may be used for both authentication and digital signatures.
certificate management	Process whereby certificates (as defined above) are generated, stored, protected, transferred, loaded, used, and destroyed.
Certificate Policy (CP)	A specialized form of administrative policy tuned to electronic transactions performed during certificate management. A Certificate Policy addresses all aspects associated with the generation, production, distribution, accounting, compromise recovery, and administration of digital certificates. Indirectly, a certificate policy can also govern the transactions conducted using a communications system protected by a certificate-based security system. By controlling critical certificate extensions, such policies and associated enforcement technology can support provision of the security services required by particular applications.
Certificate Revocation List (CRL)	A list of revoked public key certificates created and digitally signed by a Certification Authority.
Certificate Status Authority (CSA)	A trusted entity that provides on-line verification to a relying party of a subject certificate's trustworthiness, and may also provide additional attribute information for the subject certificate.
certificate-related information	Data, such as a subscriber's postal address that is not included in a certificate. May be used by a Certification Authority (CA) managing certificates.
certification	Comprehensive evaluation of the technical and non-technical security safeguards of an information system to support the accreditation process that establishes the extent to which a particular design and implementation meets a set of specified security requirements. See security control assessment.

certification analyst	The independent technical liaison for all stakeholders involved in the C&A process responsible for objectively and independently evaluating a system as part of the risk management process. Based on the security requirements documented in the security plan, performs a technical and non-technical review of potential vulnerabilities in the system and determines if the security controls (management, operational, and technical) are correctly implemented and effective.
certification authority (CA)	1. For Certification and Accreditation (C&A) (C&A Assessment): Official responsible for performing the comprehensive evaluation of the security features of an information system and determining the degree to which it meets its security requirements.
	2. For Public Key Infrastructure (PKI): A trusted third party that issues digital certificates and verifies the identity of the holder of the digital certificate.
Certification Authority Workstation (CAW)	Commercial-off-the-shelf (COTS) workstation with a trusted operating system and special purpose application software that is used to issue certificates.
certification package	Product of the certification effort documenting the detailed results of the certification activities.
Certification Practice Statement (CPS)	A listing of the practices that a Certification Authority employs in issuing, suspending, revoking, and renewing certificates and providing access to them, in accordance with specific requirements (i.e., requirements specified in this Certificate Policy, or requirements specified in a contract for services).
Certification Test and Evaluation (CT&E)	Software and hardware security tests conducted during development of an information system.
Certified TEMPEST Technical Authority (CTTA)	An experienced, technically qualified U.S. Government employee who has met established certification requirements in accordance with CNSS approved criteria and has been appointed by a U.S. Government Department or Agency to fulfill CTTA responsibilities.
certifier	Individual responsible for making a technical judgment of the system's compliance with stated requirements, identifying and assessing the risks associated with operating the system, coordinating the certification activities, and consolidating the final certification and accreditation packages.
chain of custody	A process that tracks the movement of evidence through its collection, safeguarding, and analysis lifecycle by documenting each person who handled the evidence, the date/time it was collected or transferred, and the purpose for the transfer.
chain of evidence	A process and record that shows who obtained the evidence; where and when the evidence was obtained; who secured the evidence; and who had control or possession of the evidence. The "sequencing" of the chain of evidence follows this order: collection and identification; analysis; storage; preservation; presentation in court; return to owner.
challenge and reply authentication	Prearranged procedure in which a subject requests authentication of another and the latter establishes validity with a correct reply.

10

check word	Cipher text generated by cryptographic logic to detect failures in cryptography.
checksum	Value computed on data to detect error or manipulation.
Chief Information Officer (CIO)	Agency official responsible for: 1) providing advice and other assistance to the head of the executive agency and other senior management personnel of the agency to ensure that information systems are acquired and information resources are managed in a manner that is consistent with laws, Executive Orders, directives, policies, regulations, and priorities established by the head of the agency; 2) developing, maintaining, and facilitating the implementation of a sound and integrated information system architecture for the agency; and 3) promoting the effective and efficient design and operation of all major information resources management processes for the agency, including improvements to work processes of the agency. Note: Organizations subordinate to federal agencies may use the term Chief Information Officer to denote individuals filling positions with similar security responsibilities to agency-level Chief Information Officers.
Chief Information Security Officer (CISO)	See Senior Agency Information Security Officer.
cipher	Any cryptographic system in which arbitrary symbols or groups of symbols, represent units of plain text, or in which units of plain text are rearranged, or both.
Cipher Text Auto-Key (CTAK)	Cryptographic logic that uses previous cipher text to generate a key stream.
cipher text/ciphertext	Data in its encrypted form.
ciphony (C.F.D.)	Process of enciphering audio information, resulting in encrypted speech.
claimant	An entity (user, device or process) whose assertion is to be verified using an authentication protocol.
classified information	See classified national security information.
classified information spillage	Security incident that occurs whenever classified data is spilled either onto an unclassified information system or to an information system with a lower level of classification.
classified national security information	Information that has been determined pursuant to Executive Order 13526 or any predecessor order to require protection against unauthorized disclosure and is marked to indicate its classified status when in documentary form.
clearance	Formal certification of authorization to have access to classified information other than that protected in a special access program (including SCI). Clearances are of three types: confidential, secret, and top secret. A top secret clearance permits access to top secret, secret, and confidential material; a secret clearance, to secret and confidential material; and a confidential clearance, to confidential material.

clearing

Removal of data from an information system, its storage devices, and other peripheral devices with storage capacity, in such a way that the data may not be reconstructed using common system capabilities (i.e., through the keyboard); however, the data may be reconstructed using laboratory methods.

client (C.F.D.)

Individual or process acting on behalf of an individual who makes requests of a guard or dedicated server. The client's requests to the guard or dedicated server can involve data transfer to, from, or through the guard or dedicated server.

closed security environment

Environment providing sufficient assurance that applications and equipment are protected against the introduction of malicious logic during an information system life cycle. Closed security is based upon a system's developers, operators, and maintenance personnel having sufficient clearances, authorization, and configuration control.

closed storage

Storage of classified information within an accredited facility, in General Services Administration approved secure containers, while the facility is unoccupied by authorized personnel.

cloud computing

A model for enabling on-demand network access to a shared pool of configurable IT capabilities/ resources (e.g., networks, servers, storage, applications, and services) that can be rapidly provisioned and released with minimal management effort or service provider interaction. It allows users to access technology-based services from the network cloud without knowledge of, expertise with, or control over the technology infrastructure that supports them. This cloud model is composed of five essential characteristics (on-demand self-service, ubiquitous network access, location independent resource pooling, rapid elasticity, and measured service); three service delivery models (Cloud Software as a Service (SaaS), Cloud Platform as a Service (PaaS), and Cloud Infrastructure as a Service (IaaS)); and four models for enterprise access (Private cloud, Community cloud, Public cloud and Hybrid cloud).

Note: Both the user's data and essential security services may reside in and be managed within the network cloud.

code

System of communication in which arbitrary groups of letters, numbers, or symbols represent units of plain text of varying length.

code book

Document containing plain text and code equivalents in a systematic arrangement, or a technique of machine encryption using a word substitution technique.

code group

Group of letters, numbers, or both in a code system used to represent a plain text word, phrase, or sentence.

code vocabulary

Set of plain text words, numerals, phrases, or sentences for which code equivalents are assigned in a code system.

cold site	Backup site that can be up and operational in a relatively short time span, such as a day or two. Provision of services, such as telephone lines and power, is taken care of, and the basic office furniture might be in place, but there is unlikely to be any computer equipment, even though the building might well have a network infrastructure and a room ready to act as a server room. In most cases, cold sites provide the physical location and basic services.
cold start (C.F.D.)	Procedure for initially keying crypto-equipment.
command authority	Individual responsible for the appointment of user representatives for a department, agency, or organization and their key ordering privileges.
Commercial COMSEC Evaluation Program (CCEP)	Relationship between NSA and industry in which NSA provides the COMSEC expertise (i.e., standards, algorithms, evaluations, and guidance) and industry provides design, development, and production capabilities to produce a type 1 or type 2 product. Products developed under the CCEP may include modules, subsystems, equipment, systems, and ancillary devices.
Common Access Card (CAC)	Standard identification/smart card issued by the Department of Defense that has an embedded integrated chip storing public key infrastructure (PKI) certificates.
common control	A security control that is inherited by one or more organizational information systems. See Security Control Inheritance.
Common Criteria	Governing document that provides a comprehensive, rigorous method for specifying security function and assurance requirements for products and systems.
common fill device	One of a family of devices developed to read-in, transfer, or store cryptographic key material.
Common Vulnerabilities and Exposures (CVE)	A dictionary of common names for publicly known information system vulnerabilities.
communications cover	Concealing or altering of characteristic communications patterns to hide information that could be of value to an adversary.
communications deception	Deliberate transmission, retransmission, or alteration of communications to mislead an adversary's interpretation of the communications.
communications profile	Analytic model of communications associated with an organization or activity. The model is prepared from a systematic examination of communications content and patterns, the functions they reflect, and the communications security measures applied.
Communications Security (COMSEC)	A component of Information Assurance that deals with measures and controls taken to deny unauthorized persons information derived from telecommunications and to ensure the authenticity of such telecommunications. COMSEC includes crypto security, transmission security, emissions security, and physical security of COMSEC material.

Community of Interest (COI)	A collaborative group of users who exchange information in pursuit of their shared goals, interests, missions, or business processes, and who therefore must have a shared vocabulary for the information they exchange. The group exchanges information within and between systems to include security domains.
community risk	Probability that a particular vulnerability will be exploited within an interacting population and adversely impact some members of that population.
compartmentalization	A nonhierarchical grouping of sensitive information used to control access to data more finely than with hierarchical security classification alone.
compartmented mode (C.F.D.)	Mode of operation wherein each user with direct or indirect access to a system, its peripherals, remote terminals, or remote hosts has all of the following: 1) valid security clearance for the most restricted information processed in the system, 2) formal access approval and signed nondisclosure agreements for that information which a user is to have access, and 3) valid need-to-know for information which a user is to have access.
compensating security control	A management, operational, and/or technical control (i.e., safeguard or countermeasure) employed by an organization in lieu of a recommended security control in the low, moderate, or high baselines that provides equivalent or comparable protection for an information system. NIST SP 800.53: A management, operational, and/or technical control (i.e., safeguard or countermeasure) employed by an organization in lieu of a recommended security control in the low, moderate, or high baselines described in NIST Special Publication 800-53 or in CNSS Instruction 1253, that provides equivalent or comparable protection for an information system.
compromise	Disclosure of information to unauthorized persons, or a violation of the security policy of a system in which unauthorized intentional or unintentional disclosure, modification, destruction, or loss of an object may have occurred.
compromising emanations	Unintentional signals that, if intercepted and analyzed, would disclose the information transmitted, received, handled, or otherwise processed by information system equipment. See TEMPEST.
computer abuse	Intentional or reckless misuse, alteration, disruption, or destruction of information processing resources.
computer cryptography	Use of a crypto-algorithm program by a computer to authenticate or encrypt/decrypt information.
Computer Forensics	The practice of gathering, retaining, and analyzing computer-related data for investigative purposes in a manner that maintains the integrity of the data.

Computer Incident Response Team (CIRT)	Group of individuals usually consisting of Security Analysts organized to develop, recommend, and coordinate immediate mitigation actions for containment, eradication, and recovery resulting from computer security incidents. Also called a Computer Security Incident Response Team (CSIRT) or a CIRC (Computer Incident Response Center, Computer Incident Response Capability or Cyber Incident Response Team).
Computer Network Attack (CNA)	Actions taken through the use of computer networks to disrupt, deny, degrade, or destroy information resident in computers and computer networks, or the computers and networks themselves.
Computer Network Defense (CND)	Actions taken to defend against unauthorized activity within computer networks. CND includes monitoring, detection, analysis (such as trend and pattern analysis), and response and restoration activities.
Computer Network Exploitation (CNE)	Enabling operations and intelligence collection capabilities conducted through the use of computer networks to gather data from target or adversary information systems or networks.
Computer Network Operations (CNO)	Comprised of computer network attack, computer network defense, and related computer network exploitation enabling operations.
Computer Security (COMPUSEC)	Measures and controls that ensure confidentiality, integrity, and availability of information system assets including hardware, software, firmware, and information being processed, stored, and communicated.
computer security incident	See Incident.
computer security object	A resource, tool, or mechanism used to maintain a condition of security in a computerized environment. These objects are defined in terms of attributes they possess, operations they perform or are performed on them, and their relationship with other objects.
computer security objects register	A collection of computer security object names and definitions kept by a registration authority.
computer security subsystem	Hardware/software designed to provide computer security features in a larger system environment.
computing environment (C.F.D.)	Workstation or server (host) and its operating system, peripherals, and applications.
COMSEC account	Administrative entity, identified by an account number, used to maintain accountability, custody, and control of COMSEC material.
COMSEC account audit	Examination of the holdings, records, and procedures of a COMSEC account ensuring all accountable COMSEC material is properly handled and safeguarded.

COMSEC aid	COMSEC material that assists in securing telecommunications and is required in the production, operation, or maintenance of COMSEC systems and their components. COMSEC keying material, callsign/frequency systems, and supporting documentation, such as operating and maintenance manuals, are examples of COMSEC aids.
COMSEC assembly	Group of parts, elements, subassemblies, or circuits that are removable items of COMSEC equipment.
COMSEC boundary	Definable perimeter encompassing all hardware, firmware, and software components performing critical COMSEC functions, such as key generation, handling, and storage.
COMSEC chip set	Collection of NSA approved microchips.
COMSEC control program	Computer instructions or routines controlling or affecting the externally performed functions of key generation, key distribution, message encryption/decryption, or authentication.
COMSEC custodian	Individual designated by proper authority to be responsible for the receipt, transfer, accounting, safeguarding, and destruction of COMSEC material assigned to a COMSEC account.
COMSEC demilitarization	Process of preparing COMSEC equipment for disposal by extracting all CCI, classified, or CRYPTO marked components for their secure destruction, as well as defacing and disposing of the remaining equipment hulk.
COMSEC element	Removable item of COMSEC equipment, assembly, or subassembly; normally consisting of a single piece or group of replaceable parts.
COMSEC end-item	Equipment or combination of components ready for use in a COMSEC application.
COMSEC equipment	Equipment designed to provide security to telecommunications by converting information to a form unintelligible to an unauthorized interceptor and, subsequently, by reconverting such information to its original form for authorized recipients; also, equipment designed specifically to aid in, or as an essential element of, the conversion process. COMSEC equipment includes cryptographic equipment, crypto-ancillary equipment, cryptographic production equipment, and authentication equipment.
COMSEC facility	Authorized and approved space used for generating, storing, repairing, or using COMSEC material.
COMSEC incident	Occurrence that potentially jeopardizes the security of COMSEC material or the secure electrical transmission of national security information or information governed by 10 U.S.C. Section 2315.
COMSEC insecurity	COMSEC incident that has been investigated, evaluated, and determined to jeopardize the security of COMSEC material or the secure transmission of information.
COMSEC manager	Individual who manages the COMSEC resources of an organization.

COMSEC material	Item designed to secure or authenticate telecommunications. COMSEC material includes, but is not limited to key, equipment, devices, documents, firmware, or software that embodies or describes cryptographic logic and other items that perform COMSEC functions.
COMSEC Material Control System (CMCS)	Logistics and accounting system through which COMSEC material marked "CRYPTO" is distributed, controlled, and safeguarded. Included are the COMSEC central offices of record, crypto logistic depots, and COMSEC accounts. COMSEC material other than key may be handled through the CMCS.
COMSEC modification (C.F.D.)	See information systems security equipment modification.
COMSEC module	Removable component that performs COMSEC functions in a telecommunications equipment or system.
COMSEC monitoring	Act of listening to, copying, or recording transmissions of one's own official telecommunications to analyze the degree of security.
COMSEC profile	Statement of COMSEC measures and materials used to protect a given operation, system, or organization.
COMSEC survey	Organized collection of COMSEC and communications information relative to a given operation, system, or organization.
COMSEC system data	Information required by a COMSEC equipment or system to enable it to properly handle and control key.
COMSEC training	Teaching of skills relating to COMSEC accounting, use of COMSEC aids, or installation, use, maintenance, and repair of COMSEC equipment.
Concept of Operations (CONOP)	See security concept of operations.
confidentiality	The property that information is not disclosed to system entities (users, processes, devices) unless they have been authorized to access the information. NIST SP 800.53: Preserving authorized restrictions on information access and disclosure, including means for protecting personal privacy and proprietary information.
configuration control	Process of controlling modifications to hardware, firmware, software, and documentation to protect the information system against improper modifications prior to, during, and after system implementation.
Configuration Control Board (CCB)	A group of qualified people with responsibility for the process of regulating and approving changes to hardware, firmware, software, and documentation throughout the development and operational lifecycle of an information system.
confinement channel (C.F.D.)	See covert channel.

contamination	Type of incident involving the introduction of data of one security classification or security category into data of a lower security classification or different security category.
contingency key	Key held for use under specific operational conditions or in support of specific contingency plans. See reserve keying material.
contingency plan	Management policy and procedures used to guide an enterprise response to a perceived loss of mission capability. The Contingency Plan is the first plan used by the enterprise risk managers to determine what happened, why, and what to do. It may point to the COOP or Disaster Recovery Plan for major disruptions.
Continuity of Government (COG)	A coordinated effort within the Federal Government's executive branch to ensure that national essential functions continue to be performed during a catastrophic emergency.
Continuity of Operations Plan (COOP)	Management policy and procedures used to guide an enterprise response to a major loss of enterprise capability or damage to its facilities. The COOP is the third plan needed by the enterprise risk managers and is used when the enterprise must recover (often at an alternate site) for a specified period of time. Defines the activities of individual departments and agencies and their sub-components to ensure that their essential functions are performed. This includes plans and procedures that delineate essential functions; specifies succession to office and the emergency delegation of authority; provide for the safekeeping of vital records and databases; identify alternate operating facilities; provide for interoperable communications, and validate the capability through tests, training, and exercises. See also Disaster Recovery Plan and Contingency Plan.
continuous monitoring	The process implemented to maintain a current security status for one or more information systems or for the entire suite of information systems on which the operational mission of the enterprise depends. The process includes: 1) The development of a strategy to regularly evaluate selected IA controls/metrics, 2) Recording and evaluating IA relevant events and the effectiveness of the enterprise in dealing with those events, 3) Recording changes to IA controls, or changes that affect IA risks, and 4) Publishing the current security status to enable information sharing decisions involving the enterprise.
controlled access area	Physical area (e.g., building, room, etc.) to which only authorized personnel are granted unrestricted access. All other personnel are either escorted by authorized personnel or are under continuous surveillance.
controlled access protection	Minimum set of security functionality that enforces access control on individual users and makes them accountable for their actions through login procedures, auditing of security-relevant events, and resource isolation.
controlled area	Any area or space for which the organization has confidence that the physical and procedural protections provided are sufficient to meet the requirements established for protecting the information and/or information system.

Controlled Cryptographic Item (CCI)	Secure telecommunications or information system, or associated cryptographic component, that is unclassified and handled through the COMSEC Material Control System (CMCS), an equivalent material control system, or a combination of the two that provides accountability and visibility. Such items are marked "Controlled Cryptographic Item", or, where space is limited, "CCI".
Controlled Cryptographic Item (CCI) assembly	Device embodying a cryptographic logic or other COMSEC design that NSA has approved as a Controlled Cryptographic Item (CCI). It performs the entire COMSEC function, but depends upon the host equipment to operate.
Controlled Cryptographic Item (CCI) component	Part of a Controlled Cryptographic Item (CCI) that does not perform the entire COMSEC function but depends upon the host equipment, or assembly, to complete and operate the COMSEC function.
Controlled Cryptographic Item (CCI) equipment	Telecommunications or information handling equipment that embodies a Controlled Cryptographic Item (CCI) component or CCI assembly and performs the entire COMSEC function without dependence on host equipment to operate.
controlled interface	A boundary with a set of mechanisms that enforces the security policies and controls the flow of information between interconnected information systems.
controlled space	Three-dimensional space surrounding information system equipment, within which unauthorized individuals are denied unrestricted access and are either escorted by authorized individuals or are under continuous physical or electronic surveillance.
controlling authority	Official responsible for directing the operation of a cryptonet and for managing the operational use and control of keying material assigned to the cryptonet.
cookie	Data exchanged between an HTTP server and a browser (a client of the server) to store state information on the client side and retrieve it later for server use.
cooperative key generation	Electronically exchanging functions of locally generated, random components, from which both terminals of a secure circuit construct traffic encryption key or key encryption key for use on that circuit. See per-call key.
cooperative remote rekeying	Synonymous with manual remote rekeying.
correctness proof	A mathematical proof of consistency between a specification and its implementation.
countermeasure	Actions, devices, procedures, or techniques that meet or oppose(i.e., counters) a threat, a vulnerability, or an attack by eliminating or preventing it, by minimizing the harm it can cause, or by discovering and reporting it so that corrective action can be taken. NIST SP 800-53: Actions, devices, procedures, techniques, or other measures that reduce the vulnerability of an information system. Synonymous with security controls and safeguards.

covert channel	An unauthorized communication path that manipulates a communications medium in an unexpected, unconventional or unforeseen way in order to transmit information without detection by anyone other than the entities operating the covert channel.
covert channel analysis	Determination of the extent to which the security policy model and subsequent lower-level program descriptions may allow unauthorized access to information.
covert storage channel	Covert channel involving the direct or indirect writing to a storage location by one process and the direct or indirect reading of the storage location by another process. Covert storage channels typically involve a finite resource (e.g., sectors on a disk) that is shared by two subjects at different security levels.
covert timing channel	Covert channel in which one process signals information to another process by modulating its own use of system resources (e.g., central processing unit time) in such a way that this manipulation affects the real response time observed by the second process.
credential	Evidence or testimonials that support a claim of identity or assertion of an attribute and usually are intended to be used more than once.
Credentials Service Provider (CSP)	A trusted entity that issues or registers subscriber tokens and issues electronic credentials to subscribers. The CSP may encompass registration authorities and verifiers that it operates. A CSP may be an independent third party, or may issue credentials for its own use.
critical infrastructure	System and assets, whether physical or virtual, so vital to the U.S. that the incapacity or destruction of such systems and assets would have a debilitating impact on security, national economic security, national public health or safety, or any combination of those matters.
critical security parameter	Security-related information (e.g., secret and private cryptographic keys, and authentication data such as passwords and Personal Identification Numbers (PINs)) whose disclosure or modification can compromise the security of a cryptographic module.
criticality level	Refers to the (consequences of) incorrect behavior of a system. The more serious the expected direct and indirect affects of incorrect behavior, the higher the criticality level.
cross domain capabilities	The set of functions that enable the transfer of information between security domains in accordance with the policies of the security domains involved.
Cross Domain Solution (CDS)	A form of controlled interface that provides the ability to manually and/or automatically access and/or transfer information between different security domains.
cross-certificate	A certificate used to establish a trust relationship between two Certification Authorities.

cryptanalysis	1. Operations performed in defeating cryptographic protection without an initial knowledge of the key employed in providing the protection.
	2. The study of mathematical techniques for attempting to defeat cryptographic techniques and/or information systems security. This includes the process of looking for errors or weaknesses in the implementation of an algorithm or of the algorithm itself.
cryptographic	Pertaining to, or concerned with, cryptography.
cryptographic alarm	Circuit or device that detects failures or aberrations in the logic or operation of cryptographic equipment. Crypto-alarm may inhibit transmission or may provide a visible and/or audible alarm.
cryptographic algorithm	A well-defined computational procedure that takes variable inputs, including a cryptographic key, and produces an output.
cryptographic ancillary equipment	Equipment designed specifically to facilitate efficient or reliable operation of cryptographic equipment, without performing cryptographic functions itself.
cryptographic binding	Associating two or more related elements of information using cryptographic techniques.
cryptographic component	Hardware or firmware embodiment of the cryptographic logic. A cryptographic component may be a modular assembly, a printed wiring assembly, a microcircuit, or a combination of these items.
cryptographic equipment	Equipment that embodies a cryptographic logic.
Cryptographic Ignition Key (CIK)	Device or electronic key used to unlock the secure mode of cryptographic equipment.
cryptographic initialization	Function used to set the state of a cryptographic logic prior to key generation, encryption, or other operating mode.
cryptographic logic	The embodiment of one (or more) cryptographic algorithm(s) along with alarms, checks, and other processes essential to effective and secure performance of the cryptographic process(es).
cryptographic material (*slang* CRYPTO)	COMSEC material used to secure or authenticate information.
cryptographic net	Stations holding a common key.
cryptographic period	Time span during which each key setting remains in effect.
cryptographic product	A cryptographic key (public, private, or shared) or public key certificate, used for encryption, decryption, digital signature, or signature verification; and other items, such as compromised key lists (CKL) and certificate revocation lists (CRL), obtained by trusted means from the same source which validate the authenticity of keys or certificates. Protected software which generates or regenerates keys or certificates may also be considered a cryptographic product.

cryptographic randomization	Function that randomly determines the transmit state of a cryptographic logic.
cryptographic security	Component of COMSEC resulting from the provision of technically sound cryptographic systems and their proper use.
cryptographic synchronization	Process by which a receiving decrypting cryptographic logic attains the same internal state as the transmitting encrypting logic.
cryptographic system	Associated information assurance items interacting to provide a single means of encryption or decryption.
cryptographic system analysis	Process of establishing the exploitability of a cryptographic system, normally by reviewing transmitted traffic protected or secured by the system under study.
cryptographic system evaluation	Process of determining vulnerabilities of a cryptographic system and recommending countermeasures.
cryptographic system review	Examination of a cryptographic system by the controlling authority ensuring its adequacy of design and content, continued need, and proper distribution.
cryptographic system survey	Management technique in which actual holders of a cryptographic system express opinions on the system's suitability and provide usage information for technical evaluations.
cryptographic token	A portable, user-controlled, physical device (e.g., smart card or PCMCIA card) used to store cryptographic information and possibly also perform cryptographic functions.
cryptography	Art or science concerning the principles, means, and methods for rendering plain information unintelligible and for restoring encrypted information to intelligible form.
cryptology	The mathematical science that deals with cryptanalysis and cryptography.
cyber attack	An attack, via cyberspace, targeting an enterprise's use of cyberspace for the purpose of disrupting, disabling, destroying, or maliciously controlling a computing environment/infrastructure; or destroying the integrity of the data or stealing controlled information.
cyber incident	Actions taken through the use of computer networks that result in an actual or potentially adverse effect on an information system and/or the information residing therein. See incident.
cybersecurity	The ability to protect or defend the use of cyberspace from cyber attacks.
cyberspace	A global domain within the information environment consisting of the interdependent network of information systems infrastructures including the Internet, telecommunications networks, computer systems, and embedded processors and controllers.
cyclic redundancy check	Error checking mechanism that verifies data integrity by computing a polynomial algorithm based checksum.

D

data	A subset of information in an electronic format that allows it to be retrieved or transmitted.
data aggregation	Compilation of individual data systems and data that could result in the totality of the information being classified, or classified at a higher level, or of beneficial use to an adversary.
data asset	1. Any entity that is comprised of data. For example, a database is a data asset that is comprised of data records. A data asset may be a system or application output file, database, document, or web page. A data asset also includes a service that may be provided to access data from an application. For example, a service that returns individual records from a database would be a data asset. Similarly, a web site that returns data in response to specific queries (e.g., www.weather.com) would be a data asset.

2. An information-based resource. |
data element	A basic unit of information that has a unique meaning and subcategories (data items) of distinct value. Examples of data elements include gender, race, and geographic location.
data encryption standard (DES) (C.F.D.)	Cryptographic algorithm designed for the protection of unclassified data and published by the National Institute of Standards and Technology (NIST) in Federal Information Processing Standard (FIPS) Publication 46. See Triple DES.
data flow control	Synonymous with information flow control.
data integrity	The property that data has not been changed, destroyed, or lost in an unauthorized or accidental manner.
data origin authentication	The process of verifying that the source of the data is as claimed and that the data has not been modified.
data security (C.F.D.)	Protection of data from unauthorized (accidental or intentional) modification, destruction, or disclosure. See also information security.
data transfer device (DTD)	Fill device designed to securely store, transport, and transfer electronically both COMSEC and TRANSEC key, designed to be backward compatible with the previous generation of COMSEC common fill devices, and programmable to support modern mission systems.
decertification	Revocation of the certification of an information system item or equipment for cause.
decipher	Convert enciphered text to plain text by means of a cryptographic system.
decode	Convert encoded text to plain text by means of a code.
decrypt	Generic term encompassing decode and decipher.

dedicated mode (C.F.D.)	Information systems security mode of operation wherein each user, with direct or indirect access to the system, its peripherals, remote terminals, or remote hosts, has all of the following: 1) valid security clearance for all information within the system, 2) formal access approval and signed nondisclosure agreements for all the information stored and/or processed (including all compartments, subcompartments, and/or special access programs), and 3) valid need-to-know for all information contained within the information system. When in the dedicated security mode, a system is specifically and exclusively dedicated to and controlled for the processing of one particular type or classification of information, either for full-time operation or for a specified period of time.
default classification	Classification reflecting the highest classification being processed in an information system. Default classification is included in the caution statement affixed to an object.
Defense-in-Breadth	A planned, systematic set of multi-disciplinary activities that seek to identify, manage, and reduce risk of exploitable vulnerabilities at every stage of the system, network, or sub-component lifecycle (system, network, or product design and development; manufacturing; packaging; assembly; system integration; distribution; operations; maintenance; and retirement).
Defense-in-Depth	Information Security strategy integrating people, technology, and operations capabilities to establish variable barriers across multiple layers and missions of the organization.
degauss	Procedure to reduce the magnetic flux to virtual zero by applying a reverse magnetizing field. Also called demagnetizing.
delegated development program (C.F.D.)	INFOSEC program in which the Director, NSA, delegates, on a case-by-case basis, the development and/or production of an entire telecommunications product, including the INFOSEC portion, to a lead department or agency.
deleted file	A file that has been logically, but not necessarily physically, erased from the operating system, perhaps to eliminate potentially incriminating evidence. Deleting files does not always necessarily eliminate the possibility of recovering all or part of the original data.
Delivery-Only Client (DOC)	A configuration of a client node that enables a DOA agent to access a primary services node (PRSN) to retrieve KMI products and access KMI services. A DOC consists of a client platform but does not include an AKP.
Demilitarized Zone (DMZ)	Perimeter network segment that is logically between internal and external networks. Its purpose is to enforce the internal network's Information Assurance policy for external information exchange and to provide external, untrusted sources with restricted access to releasable information while shielding the internal networks from outside attacks.
Denial of Service (DoS)	The prevention of authorized access to resources or the delaying of time-critical operations. (Time-critical may be milliseconds or it may be hours, depending upon the service provided.)

descriptive top-level specification (DTLS) (C.F.D.)	A natural language descriptive of a system's security requirements, an informal design notation, or a combination of the two.
Designated Approval Authority (DAA)	Official with the authority to formally assume responsibility for operating a system at an acceptable level of risk. This term is synonymous with authorizing official, designated accrediting authority, and delegated accrediting authority.
device distribution profile	An approval-based Access Control List (ACL) for a specific product that 1) names the user devices in a specific KMI Operating Account (KOA) to which primary services node s (PRSNs) distribute the product and 2) states conditions of distribution for each device.
device registration manager	The management role that is responsible for performing activities related to registering users that are devices.
dial back (C.F.D.)	Synonymous with call back.
digital signature	Cryptographic process used to assure data object originator authenticity, data integrity, and time stamping for prevention of replay.
direct shipment (C.F.D)	Shipment of COMSEC material directly from NSA to user COMSEC accounts.
Disaster Recovery Plan (DRP)	Management policy and procedures used to guide an enterprise response to a major loss of enterprise capability or damage to its facilities. The DRP is the second plan needed by the enterprise risk managers and is used when the enterprise must recover (at its original facilities) from a loss of capability over a period of hours or days. See Continuity of Operations Plan and Contingency Plan.
Discretionary Access Control (DAC)	A means of restricting access to objects (e.g., files, data entities) based on the identity and need-to-know of subjects (e.g., users, processes) and/or groups to which the object belongs. The controls are discretionary in the sense that a subject with a certain access permission is capable of passing that permission (perhaps indirectly) on to any other subject (unless restrained by mandatory access control).
disruption	An unplanned event that causes the general system or major application to be inoperable for an unacceptable length of time (e.g., minor or extended power outage, extended unavailable network, or equipment or facility damage or destruction).
Distinguished Name (DN)	A unique name or character string that unambiguously identifies an entity according to the hierarchical naming conventions of X.500 directory service.
distinguishing identifier	Information which unambiguously distinguishes an entity in the authentication process.
Distributed Denial of Service (DDoS)	A Denial of Service technique that uses numerous hosts to perform the attack.

domain	An environment or context that includes a set of system resources and a set of system entities that have the right to access the resources as defined by a common security policy, security model, or security architecture. See also security domain.
drop accountability (C.F.D.)	Procedure under which a COMSEC account custodian initially receipts for COMSEC material, and provides no further accounting for it to its central office of record. Local accountability of the COMSEC material may continue to be required. See accounting legend code.

E

e-government (e-gov)	The use by the U.S. Government of web-based Internet applications and other information technology.
electronic authentication (e-authentication)	The process of establishing confidence in user identities electronically presented to an information system.
electronic business (e-business)	Doing business online.
electronic credentials	Digital documents used in authentication that bind an identity or an attribute to a subscriber's token.
Electronic Key Management System (EKMS)	Interoperable collection of systems being developed by services and agencies of the U.S. Government to automate the planning, ordering, generating, distributing, storing, filling, using, and destroying of electronic key and management of other types of COMSEC material.
electronic messaging services	Services providing interpersonal messaging capability; meeting specific functional, management, and technical requirements; and yielding a business-quality electronic mail service suitable for the conduct of official government business.
electronic signature	The process of applying any mark in electronic form with the intent to sign a data object. See also digital signature.
electronically generated key	Key generated in a COMSEC device by introducing (either mechanically or electronically) a seed key into the device and then using the seed, together with a software algorithm stored in the device, to produce the desired key.
emanations security (EMSEC)	Protection resulting from measures taken to deny unauthorized individuals information derived from intercept and analysis of compromising emissions from crypto-equipment or an information system. See TEMPEST.
embedded computer (C.F.D.)	Computer system that is an integral part of a larger system.
embedded cryptographic system (C.F.D.)	Cryptosystem performing or controlling a function as an integral element of a larger system or subsystem.
embedded cryptography (C.F.D.)	Cryptography engineered into an equipment or system whose basic function is not cryptographic.

encipher	Convert plain text to cipher text by means of a cryptographic system.
enclave	Collection of information systems connected by one or more internal networks under the control of a single authority and security policy. The systems may be structured by physical proximity or by function, independent of location.
enclave boundary	Point at which an enclave's internal network service layer connects to an external network's service layer, i.e., to another enclave or to a Wide Area Network (WAN).
encode	Convert plain text to cipher text by means of a code.
encrypt (C.F.D.)	Generic term encompassing encipher and encode.
encryption	The process of changing plaintext into ciphertext for the purpose of security or privacy.
encryption algorithm	Set of mathematically expressed rules for rendering data unintelligible by executing a series of conversions controlled by a key.
End Cryptographic Unit (ECU)	Device that 1) performs cryptographic functions, 2) typically is part of a larger system for which the device provides security services, and 3) from the viewpoint of a supporting security infrastructure (e.g., a key management system) is the lowest level of identifiable component with which a management transaction can be conducted.
end-item accounting	Accounting for all the accountable components of a COMSEC equipment configuration by a single short title.
end-to-end encryption	Encryption of information at its origin and decryption at its intended destination without intermediate decryption.
end-to-end security	Safeguarding information in an information system from point of origin to point of destination.
enrollment manager	The management role that is responsible for assigning user identities to management and non-management roles.
enterprise	An organization with a defined mission/goal and a defined boundary, using information systems to execute that mission, and with responsibility for managing its own risks and performance. An enterprise may consist of all or some of the following business aspects: acquisition, program management, financial management (e.g., budgets), human resources, security, and information systems, information and mission management.
Enterprise Architecture (EA)	The description of an enterprise's entire set of information systems: how they are configured, how they are integrated, how they interface to the external environment at the enterprise's boundary, how they are operated to support the enterprise mission, and how they contribute to the enterprise's overall security posture.

enterprise risk management	The methods and processes used by an enterprise to manage risks to its mission and to establish the trust necessary for the enterprise to support shared missions. It involves the identification of mission dependencies on enterprise capabilities, the identification and prioritization of risks due to defined threats, the implementation of countermeasures to provide both a static risk posture and an effective dynamic response to active threats; and it assesses enterprise performance against threats and adjusts countermeasures as necessary.
enterprise service	A set of one or more computer applications and middleware systems hosted on computer hardware that provides standard information systems capabilities to end users and hosted mission applications and services.
entrapment (C.F.D.)	Deliberate planting of apparent flaws in an information system for the purpose of detecting attempted penetrations.
environment (C.F.D.)	Aggregate of external procedures, conditions, and objects affecting the development, operation, and maintenance of an information system.
erasure	Process intended to render magnetically stored information irretrievable by normal means.
error detection code	A code computed from data and comprised of redundant bits of information designed to detect, but not correct, unintentional changes in the data.
Evaluated Products List (EPL)	List of validated products that have been successfully evaluated under the National Information Assurance Partnership (NIAP) Common Criteria Evaluation and Validation Scheme (CCEVS).
Evaluation Assurance Level (EAL)	Set of assurance requirements that represent a point on the Common Criteria predefined assurance scale.
event	Any observable occurrence in a system and/or network. Events sometimes provide indication that an incident is occurring.
Executive Agency	An executive department specified in 5 U.S.C., Sec. 101; a military department specified in 5 U.S.C., Sec. 102; an independent establishment as defined in 5 U.S.C., Sec. 104(1); and a wholly owned Government corporation fully subject to the provisions of 31 U.S.C., Chapter 91.
exercise key (C.F.D.)	Cryptographic key material used exclusively to safeguard communications transmitted over-the-air during military or organized civil training exercises.
exploitable channel	Channel that allows the violation of the security policy governing an information system and is usable or detectable by subjects external to the trusted computing base. See also covert channel.
external information system (or component)	An information system or component of an information system that is outside of the authorization boundary established by the organization and for which the organization typically has no direct control over the application of required security controls or the assessment of security control effectiveness.

external information system service	An information system service that is implemented outside of the authorization boundary of the organizational information system (i.e., a service that is used by, but not a part of, the organizational information system) and for which the organization typically has no direct control over the application of required security controls or the assessment of security control effectiveness.
external network	A network not controlled by the organization.
extraction resistance (C.F.D.)	Capability of crypto-equipment or secure telecommunications equipment to resist efforts to extract key.
extranet	A private network that uses Web technology, permitting the sharing of portions of an enterprise's information or operations with suppliers, vendors, partners, customers, or other enterprises.

F

fail safe	Automatic protection of programs and/or processing systems when hardware or software failure is detected.
fail soft (C.F.D.)	Selective termination of affected nonessential processing when hardware or software failure is determined to be imminent.
failover	The capability to switch over automatically (typically without human intervention or warning) to a redundant or standby information system upon the failure or abnormal termination of the previously active system.
failure access	Type of incident in which unauthorized access to data results from hardware or software failure.
failure control	Methodology used to detect imminent hardware or software failure and provide fail safe or fail soft recovery.
false acceptance	In biometrics, the instance of a security system incorrectly verifying or identifying an unauthorized person. It typically is considered the most serious of biometric security errors as it gives unauthorized users access to systems that expressly are trying to keep them out.
False Acceptance Rate (FAR)	The measure of the likelihood that the biometric security system will incorrectly accept an access attempt by an unauthorized user. A system's false acceptance rate typically is stated as the ratio of the number of false acceptances divided by the number of identification attempts.
false rejection	In biometrics, the instance of a security system failing to verify or identify an authorized person. It does not necessarily indicate a flaw in the biometric system; for example, in a fingerprint-based system, an incorrectly aligned finger on the scanner or dirt on the scanner can result in the scanner misreading the fingerprint, causing a false rejection of the authorized user.
False Rejection Rate (FRR)	The measure of the likelihood that the biometric security system will incorrectly reject an access attempt by an authorized user. A system's false rejection rate typically is stated as the ratio of the number of false rejections divided by the number of identification attempts.

Federal Bridge Certification Authority (FBCA)	The Federal Bridge Certification Authority consists of a collection of Public Key Infrastructure components (Certificate Authorities, Directories, Certificate Policies and Certificate Practice Statements) that are used to provide peer-to-peer interoperability among agency principal certification authorities.
Federal Enterprise Architecture (FEA)	A business-based framework for government-wide improvement developed by the Office of Management and Budget that is intended to facilitate efforts to transform the federal government to one that is citizen-centered, results-oriented, and market-based.
Federal Information Processing Standard (FIPS)	A standard for adoption and use by Federal agencies that has been developed within the Information Technology Laboratory and published by the National Institute of Standards and Technology, a part of the U.S. Department of Commerce. A FIPS covers some topic in information technology in order to achieve a common level of quality or some level of interoperability.
Federal Information Security Management Act (FISMA)	A statute (Title III, P.L. 107-347) that requires agencies to assess risk to information systems and provide information security protections commensurate with the risk. FISMA also requires that agencies integrate information security into their capital planning and enterprise architecture processes, conduct annual information systems security reviews of all programs and systems, and report the results of those reviews to OMB.
federal information system	An information system used or operated by an executive agency, by a contractor of an executive agency, or by another organization on behalf of an executive agency.
file protection	Aggregate of processes and procedures designed to inhibit unauthorized access, contamination, elimination, modification, or destruction of a file or any of its contents.
file security (C.F.D.)	Means by which access to computer files is limited to authorized users only.
fill device	COMSEC item used to transfer or store key in electronic form or to insert key into cryptographic equipment.
FIREFLY	Key management protocol based on public key cryptography.
firewall	A hardware/software capability that limits access between networks and/or systems in accordance with a specific security policy.
firmware	Computer programs and data stored in hardware - typically in read-only memory (ROM) or programmable read-only memory (PROM) - such that the programs and data cannot be dynamically written or modified during execution of the programs.
fixed COMSEC facility	COMSEC facility located in an immobile structure or aboard a ship.
flaw (C.F.D.)	Error of commission, omission, or oversight in an information system that may allow protection mechanisms to be bypassed.

flaw hypothesis methodology (C.F.D.)	System analysis and penetration technique in which the specification and documentation for an information system are analyzed to produce a list of hypothetical flaws. This list is prioritized on the basis of the estimated probability that a flaw exists, on the ease of exploiting it, and on the extent of control or compromise it would provide. The prioritized list is used to perform penetration testing of a system.
flooding	An attack that attempts to cause a failure in a system by providing more input than the system can process properly.
forensic copy	An accurate bit-for-bit reproduction of the information contained on an electronic device or associated media, whose validity and integrity has been verified using an accepted algorithm.
forensics	The practice of gathering, retaining, and analyzing computer-related data for investigative purposes in a manner that maintains the integrity of the data.
formal access approval	A formalization of the security determination for authorizing access to a specific type of classified or sensitive information, based on specified access requirements, a determination of the individual's security eligibility and a determination that the individual's official duties require the individual be provided access to the information.
formal development methodology (C.F.D.)	Software development strategy that proves security methodology design specifications.
formal method (C.F.D.)	Mathematical argument which verifies that the system satisfies a mathematically described security policy.
formal security policy (C.F.D.)	Mathematically precise statement of a security policy.
frequency hopping	Repeated switching of frequencies during radio transmission according to a specified algorithm, to minimize unauthorized interception or jamming of telecommunications.
full maintenance (C.F.D.)	Complete diagnostic repair, modification, and overhaul of COMSEC equipment, including repair of defective assemblies by piece part replacement. See limited maintenance.
functional testing (C.F.D.)	Segment of security testing in which advertised security mechanisms of an information system are tested under operational conditions.

G

gateway	Interface providing compatibility between networks by converting transmission speeds, protocols, codes, or security measures.

General Support Systems (GSS)	An interconnected set of information resources under the same direct management control which shares common functionality. A system normally includes hardware, software, information, data, applications, communications, and people. A system can be, for example, a local area network (LAN) including smart terminals that supports a branch office, an agency-wide backbone, a communications network, a departmental data processing center including its operating system and utilities, a tactical radio network, or a shared information processing service organization (IPSO).
Global Information Grid (GIG)	The globally interconnected, end-to-end set of information capabilities for collecting, processing, storing, disseminating, and managing information on demand to warfighters, policy makers, and support personnel. The GIG includes owned and leased communications and computing systems and services, software (including applications), data, security services, other associated services, and National Security Systems. Non-GIG IT includes stand-alone, self-contained, or embedded IT that is not, and will not be, connected to the enterprise network.
Global Information Infrastructure (GII) (C.F.D.)	Worldwide interconnections of the information systems of all countries, international and multinational organizations, and international commercial communications.
group authenticator	Used, sometimes in addition to a sign-on authenticator, to allow access to specific data or functions that may be shared by all members of a particular group.
Guard (system)	A mechanism limiting the exchange of information between information systems or subsystems.

H

hacker	Unauthorized user who attempts to or gains access to an information system.
handshaking procedures	Dialogue process between two information systems for synchronizing, identifying, and authenticating themselves to one another.
hard copy key	Physical keying material, such as printed key lists, punched or printed key tapes, or programmable, read-only memories (PROM).
hardware	The physical components of an information system. See software and firmware.
hardwired key	Permanently installed key.
hash total (C.F.D.)	Value computed on data to detect error or manipulation. See checksum.
hash value/result	See message digest.
Hash-Based Message Authentication Code (HMAC)	A message authentication code that uses a cryptographic key in conjunction with a hash function.

hashing	The process of using a mathematical algorithm against data to produce a numeric value that is representative of that data.
hashword (C.F.D.)	Memory address containing hash total.
high assurance guard (C.F.D.)	A guard that has two basic functional capabilities: a Message Guard and a Directory Guard. The Message Guard provides filter service for message traffic traversing the Guard between adjacent security domains. The Director Guard provides filter service for directory access and updates traversing the Guard between adjacent security domains.
high impact	The loss of confidentiality, integrity, or availability that could be expected to have a severe or catastrophic adverse effect on organizational operations, organizational assets, individuals, other organizations, or the national security interests of the United States; (i.e., 1) causes a severe degradation in mission capability to an extent and duration that the organization is able to perform its primary functions, but the effectiveness of the functions is significantly reduced; 2) results in major damage to organizational assets; 3) results in major financial loss; or 4) results in severe or catastrophic harm to individuals involving loss of life or serious life threatening injuries.)
high-impact system	An information system in which at least one security objective (i.e., confidentiality, integrity, or availability) is assigned a potential impact value of high.
honeypot	A system (e.g., a web server) or system resource (e.g., a file on a server) that is designed to be attractive to potential crackers and intruders and has no authorized users other than its administrators.
hot site	Backup site that includes phone systems with the phone lines already connected. Networks will also be in place, with any necessary routers and switches plugged in and turned on. Desks will have desktop PCs installed and waiting, and server areas will be replete with the necessary hardware to support business-critical functions. Within a few hours, a hot site can become a fully functioning element of an organization.
hybrid security control	A security control that is implemented in an information system in part as a common control and in part as a system-specific control. See Common Control and System-Specific Security Control.

I

IA architecture	A description of the structure and behavior for an enterprise's security processes, information security systems, personnel and organizational sub-units, showing their alignment with the enterprise's mission and strategic plans.
IA infrastructure	The underlying security framework that lies beyond an enterprise's defined boundary, but supports its IA and IA-enabled products, its security posture and its risk management plan.

IA product	Product whose primary purpose is to provide security services (e.g., confidentiality, authentication, integrity, access control, non-repudiation of data); correct known vulnerabilities; and/or provide layered defense against various categories of non-authorized or malicious penetrations of information systems or networks.
IA-enabled information technology product (C.F.D.)	Product or technology whose primary role is not security, but which provides security services as an associated feature of its intended operating capabilities. Examples include such products as security-enabled web browsers, screening routers, trusted operating systems, and security-enabled messaging systems.
IA-enabled product	Product whose primary role is not security, but provides security services as an associated feature of its intended operating capabilities. Note: Examples include such products as security-enabled web browsers, screening routers, trusted operating systems, and security enabling messaging systems.
identification	An act or process that presents an identifier to a system so that the system can recognize a system entity (e.g., user, process, or device) and distinguish that entity from all others.
identifier	A data object - often, a printable, non-blank character string - that definitively represents a specific identity of a system entity, distinguishing that identity from all others.
identity	The set of attribute values (i.e., characteristics) by which an entity is recognizable and that, within the scope of an identity manager's responsibility, is sufficient to distinguish that entity from any other entity.
identity registration	The process of making a person's identity known to the Personal Identity Verification (PIV) system, associating a unique identifier with that identity, and collecting and recording the person's relevant attributes into the system.
identity token	Smart card, metal key, or other physical object used to authenticate identity.
identity validation (C.F.D.)	Tests enabling an information system to authenticate users or resources.
identity-based access control	Access control based on the identity of the user (typically relayed as a characteristic of the process acting on behalf of that user) where access authorizations to specific objects are assigned based on user identity.
imitative communications deception (C.F.D.)	Introduction of deceptive messages or signals into an adversary's telecommunications signals. See communications deception and manipulative communications deception.
impact level	The magnitude of harm that can be expected to result from the consequences of unauthorized disclosure of information, unauthorized modification of information, unauthorized destruction of information, or loss of information or information system availability.
implant	Electronic device or electronic equipment modification designed to gain unauthorized interception of information-bearing emanations.

34

inadvertent disclosure	Type of incident involving accidental exposure of information to an individual not authorized access.
incident	An assessed occurrence that actually or potentially jeopardizes the confidentiality, integrity, or availability of an information system; or the information the system processes, stores, or transmits; or that constitutes a violation or imminent threat of violation of security policies, security procedures, or acceptable use policies.
incident response plan	The documentation of a predetermined set of instructions or procedures to detect, respond to, and limit consequences of an incident against an organization's IT systems(s).
incomplete parameter checking (C.F.D.)	System flaw that exists when the operating system does not check all parameters fully for accuracy and consistency, thus making the system vulnerable to penetration.
Independent Validation Authority (IVA)	Entity that reviews the soundness of independent tests and system compliance with all stated security controls and risk mitigation actions. IVAs will be designated by the Authorizing Official as needed.
Independent Verification & Validation (IV&V)	A comprehensive review, analysis, and testing, (software and/or hardware) performed by an objective third party to confirm (i.e., verify) that the requirements are correctly defined, and to confirm (i.e., validate) that the system correctly implements the required functionality and security requirements.
indicator	Recognized action, specific, generalized, or theoretical, that an adversary might be expected to take in preparation for an attack.
individual accountability	Ability to associate positively the identity of a user with the time, method, and degree of access to an information system.
informal security policy (C.F.D.)	Natural language description, possibly supplemented by mathematical arguments, demonstrating the correspondence of the functional specification to the high-level design.
information	Any communication or representation of knowledge such as facts, data, or opinions in any medium or form, including textual, numerical, graphic, cartographic, narrative, or audiovisual. NIST SP 800-53: An instance of an information type.
Information Assurance (IA)	Measures that protect and defend information and information systems by ensuring their availability, integrity, authentication, confidentiality, and non-repudiation. These measures include providing for restoration of information systems by incorporating protection, detection, and reaction capabilities.
Information Assurance (IA) professional	Individual who works IA issues and has real world experience plus appropriate IA training and education commensurate with their level of IA responsibility.

Information Assurance Component (IAC)	An application (hardware and/or software) that provides one or more Information Assurance capabilities in support of the overall security and operational objectives of a system.
Information Assurance Manager (IAM)	See information systems security manager.
Information Assurance Officer (IAO)	See information systems security officer.
Information Assurance Vulnerability Alert (IAVA)	Notification that is generated when an Information Assurance vulnerability may result in an immediate and potentially severe threat to DoD systems and information; this alert requires corrective action because of the severity of the vulnerability risk.
information domain	A three-part concept for information sharing, independent of, and across information systems and security domains that 1) identifies information sharing participants as individual members, 2) contains shared information objects, and 3) provides a security policy that identifies the roles and privileges of the members and the protections required for the information objects.
information environment	Aggregate of individuals, organizations, and/or systems that collect, process, or disseminate information, also included is the information itself.
information flow control	Procedure to ensure that information transfers within an information system are not made in violation of the security policy.
information management	The planning, budgeting, manipulating, and controlling of information throughout its life cycle.
information operations (IO)	The integrated employment of the core capabilities of electronic warfare, computer network operations, psychological operations, military deception, and operations security, in concert with specified supporting and related capabilities, to influence, disrupt, corrupt, or usurp adversarial human and automated decision making process, information, and information systems while protecting our own.
information owner	Official with statutory or operational authority for specified information and responsibility for establishing the controls for its generation, classification, collection, processing, dissemination, and disposal. See also information steward. NIST 800-53: Official with statutory or operational authority for specified information and responsibility for establishing the controls for its generation, collection, processing, dissemination, and disposal.
information resources	Information and related resources, such as personnel, equipment, funds, and information technology.
Information Resources Management (IRM)	The planning, budgeting, organizing, directing, training, controlling, and management activities associated with the burden, collection, creation, use, and dissemination of information by agencies.

information security	The protection of information and information systems from unauthorized access, use, disclosure, disruption, modification, or destruction in order to provide confidentiality, integrity, and availability.
information security policy	Aggregate of directives, regulations, rules, and practices that prescribe how an organization manages, protects, and distributes information.
Information Sharing Environment (ISE)	1. An approach that facilitates the sharing of terrorism and homeland security information. 2. ISE in its broader application enables those in a trusted partnership to share, discover, and access controlled information.
information steward	An agency official with statutory or operational authority for specified information and responsibility for establishing the controls for its generation, collection, processing, dissemination, and disposal.
Information System (IS)	A discrete set of information resources organized for the collection, processing, maintenance, use, sharing, dissemination, or disposition of information. Note: Information systems also include specialized systems such as industrial/process controls systems, telephone switching and private branch exchange (PBX) systems, and environmental control systems.
information system life cycle	The phases through which an information system passes, typically characterized as initiation, development, operation, and termination (i.e., sanitization, disposal and/or destruction).
Information Systems Security (INFOSEC) (C.F.D.)	Protection of information systems against unauthorized access to or modification of information, whether in storage, processing or transit, and against the denial of service to authorized users, including those measures necessary to detect, document, and counter such threats. See Information Assurance.
Information Systems Security Engineer (ISSE)	Individual assigned responsibility for conducting information system security engineering activities.
Information Systems Security Engineering (ISSE)	Process of capturing and refining information protection requirements to ensure their integration into information systems acquisition and information systems development through purposeful security design or configuration.
information systems security equipment modification (C.F.D.)	Modification of any fielded hardware, firmware, software, or portion thereof, under NSA configuration control. There are three classes of modifications: mandatory (to include human safety); optional/special mission modifications; and repair actions. These classes apply to elements, subassemblies, equipment, systems, and software packages performing functions such as key generation, key distribution, message encryption, decryption, authentication, or those mechanisms necessary to satisfy security policy, labeling, identification, or accountability.
Information Systems Security Manager (ISSM)	Individual responsible for the information assurance of a program, organization, system, or enclave.

Information Systems Security Officer (ISSO)	Individual assigned responsibility for maintaining the appropriate operational security posture for an information system or program.
information systems security product (C.F.D.)	Item (chip, module, assembly, or equipment), technique, or service that performs or relates to information systems security.
Information Technology (IT)	Any equipment or interconnected system or subsystem of equipment that is used in the automatic acquisition, storage, manipulation, management, movement, control, display, switching, interchange, transmission, or reception of data or information by the executive agency. For purposes of the preceding sentence, equipment is used by an executive agency if the equipment is used by the executive agency directly or is used by a contractor under a contract with the executive agency which 1) requires the use of such equipment or 2) requires the use, to a significant extent, of such equipment in the performance of a service or the furnishing of a product. The term information technology includes computers, ancillary equipment, software, firmware and similar procedures, services (including support services), and related resources.
information type	A specific category of information (e.g., privacy, medical, proprietary, financial, investigative, contractor sensitive, security management), defined by an organization or in some instances, by a specific law, Executive Order, directive, policy, or regulation.
information value	A qualitative measure of the importance of the information based upon factors such as: level of robustness of the Information Assurance controls allocated to the protection of information based upon: mission criticality, the sensitivity (e.g., classification and compartmentalization) of the information, releasability to other countries, perishability/longevity of the information (e.g., short life data versus long life intelligence source data), and potential impact of loss of confidentiality and integrity and/or availability of the information.
inheritance	See security control inheritance.
initialize (C.F.D.)	Setting the state of a cryptographic logic prior to key generation, encryption, or other operating mode.
inside(r) threat	An entity with authorized access (i.e., within the security domain) that has the potential to harm an information system or enterprise through destruction, disclosure, modification of data, and/or denial of service.
inspectable space (C.F.D.)	Three dimensional space surrounding equipment that processes classified and/or sensitive information within which TEMPEST exploitation is not considered practical or where legal authority to identify and remove a potential TEMPEST exploitation exists. Synonymous with zone of control.
integrity	The property whereby an entity has not been modified in an unauthorized manner. NIST 800-53: Guarding against improper information modification or destruction, and includes ensuring information non-repudiation and authenticity.
integrity check value	Checksum capable of detecting modification of an information system.

38

intellectual property	Creations of the mind such as musical, literary, and artistic works; inventions; and symbols, names, images, and designs used in commerce, including copyrights, trademarks, patents, and related rights. Under intellectual property law, the holder of one of these abstract "properties" has certain exclusive rights to the creative work, commercial symbol, or invention by which it is covered.
Interconnection Security Agreement (ISA)	A document that regulates security-relevant aspects of an intended connection between an agency and an external system. It regulates the security interface between any two systems operating under two different distinct authorities. It includes a variety of descriptive, technical, procedural, and planning information. It is usually preceded by a formal MOA/MOU that defines high-level roles and responsibilities in management of a cross-domain connection.
interface	Common boundary between independent systems or modules where interactions take place.
interface control document (C.F.D.)	Technical document describing interface controls and identifying the authorities and responsibilities for ensuring the operation of such controls. This document is baselined during the preliminary design review and is maintained throughout the information system lifecycle.
Interim Approval To Operate (IATO)	Temporary authorization granted by a DAA for an information system to process information based on preliminary results of a security evaluation of the system. (To be replaced by ATO and POA&M)
Interim Approval To Test (IATT)	Temporary authorization to test an information system in a specified operational information environment within the timeframe and under the conditions or constraints enumerated in the written authorization.
internal network	A network where 1) the establishment, maintenance, and provisioning of security controls are under the direct control of organizational employees or contractors; or 2) cryptographic encapsulation or similar security technology implemented between organization-controlled endpoints provides the same effect (at least with regard to confidentiality and integrity). An internal network is typically organization-owned, yet may be organization-controlled while not being organization-owned.
internal security controls	Hardware, firmware, or software features within an information system that restrict access to resources to only authorized subjects.
Internet	The Internet is the single, interconnected, worldwide system of commercial, governmental, educational, and other computer networks that share (a) the protocol suite specified by the IAB and (b) the name and address spaces managed by the Internet Corporation for Assigned Names and Numbers (ICANN).
Internet Protocol (IP)	Standard protocol for transmission of data from source to destinations in packet-switched communications networks and interconnected systems of such networks.
intranet	A private network that is employed within the confines of a given enterprise (e.g., internal to a business or agency).

intrusion	Unauthorized act of bypassing the security mechanisms of a system.
Intrusion Detection Systems (IDS)	Hardware or software products that gather and analyze information from various areas within a computer or a network to identify possible security breaches, which include both intrusions (attacks from outside the organizations) and misuse (attacks from with the organizations).
Intrusion Detection Systems (IDS), (host-based)	IDSs which operate on information collected from within an individual computer system. This vantage point allows host-based IDSs to determine exactly which processes and user accounts are involved in a particular attack on the Operating System. Furthermore, unlike network-based IDSs, host-based IDSs can more readily "see" the intended outcome of an attempted attack, because they can directly access and monitor the data files and system processes usually targeted by attacks.
Intrusion Detection Systems (IDS), (network-based)	IDSs which detect attacks by capturing and analyzing network packets. Listening on a network segment or switch, one network-based IDS can monitor the network traffic affecting multiple hosts that are connected to the network segment.
Intrusion Prevention System (IPS)	System that can detect an intrusive activity and can also attempt to stop the activity, ideally before it reaches its targets.
IP Security (IPSec)	Suite of protocols for securing Internet Protocol (IP) communications at the network layer, layer 3 of the OSI model by authenticating and/or encrypting each IP packet in a data stream. IPSec also includes protocols for cryptographic key establishment.
IT security awareness and training program	Explains proper rules of behavior for the use of agency information systems and information. The program communicates IT security policies and procedures that need to be followed. (i.e., NSTISSD 501, NIST SP 800-50)

J

jamming	An attack that attempts to interfere with the reception of broadcast communications.

K

key	A numerical value used to control cryptographic operations, such as decryption, encryption, signature generation, or signature verification.
Key Distribution Center (KDC)	COMSEC facility generating and distributing key in electronic form.
key escrow	1. The processes of managing (e.g., generating, storing, transferring, auditing) the two components of a cryptographic key by two key component holders.
	2. A key recovery technique for storing knowledge of a cryptographic key, or parts thereof, in the custody of one or more third parties called "escrow agents," so that the key can be recovered and used in specified circumstances.

key escrow system	A system that entrusts the two components comprising a cryptographic key (e.g., a device unique key) to two key component holders (also called "escrow agents").
key establishment	The process by which cryptographic keys are securely established among cryptographic modules using key transport and/or key agreement procedures. See key distribution.
key exchange	Process of exchanging public keys (and other information) in order to establish secure communications.
key generation material	Random numbers, pseudo-random numbers, and cryptographic parameters used in generating cryptographic keys.
key list	Printed series of key settings for a specific cryptonet. Key lists may be produced in list, pad, or printed tape format.
key loader	A self-contained unit that is capable of storing at least one plaintext or encrypted cryptographic key or a component of a key that can be transferred, upon request, into a cryptographic module.
key management	The activities involving the handling of cryptographic keys and other related security parameters (e.g., IVs and passwords) during the entire life cycle of the keys, including their generation, storage, establishment, entry and output, and zeroization.
key management device	A unit that provides for secure electronic distribution of encryption keys to authorized users.
Key Management Infrastructure (KMI)	All parts – computer hardware, firmware, software, and other equipment and its documentation; facilities that house the equipment and related functions; and companion standards, policies, procedures, and doctrine that form the system that manages and supports the ordering and delivery of cryptographic material and related information products and services to users.
key pair	A public key and its corresponding private key; a key pair is used with a public key algorithm.
Key Production Key (KPK) (C.F.D.)	Key used to initialize a keystream generator for the production of other electronically generated key.
key recovery	Mechanisms and processes that allow authorized parties to retrieve the cryptographic key used for data confidentiality.
key stream	Sequence of symbols (or their electrical or mechanical equivalents) produced in a machine or auto-manual cryptosystem to combine with plain text to produce cipher text, control transmission security processes, or produce key.
key tag	Identification information associated with certain types of electronic key.
key tape	Punched or magnetic tape containing key. Printed key in tape form is referred to as a key list.

key transport	The secure transport of cryptographic keys from one cryptographic module to another module.
key updating	Irreversible cryptographic process for modifying key.
Key-Auto-Key (KAK)	Cryptographic logic using previous key to produce key.
Keyed Hash-Based Message Authentication Code (HMAC)	A message authentication code that uses a cryptographic key in conjunction with a hash function.
Key-Encryption-Key (KEK)	Key that encrypts or decrypts other key for transmission or storage.
keying material	Key, code, or authentication information in physical, electronic, or magnetic form.
keystroke monitoring	The process used to view or record both the keystrokes entered by a computer user and the computer's response during an interactive session. Keystroke monitoring is usually considered a special case of audit trails.
KMI Operating Account (KOA)	A KMI business relationship that is established 1) to manage the set of user devices that are under the control of a specific KMI customer organization and 2) to control the distribution of KMI products to those devices.
KMI Protected Channel (KPC)	A KMI Communication Channel that provides 1) Information Integrity Service; 2) either Data Origin Authentication Service or Peer Entity Authentication Service, as is appropriate to the mode of communications; and 3) optionally, Information Confidentiality Service.
KMI-Aware Device	A user device that has a user identity for which the registration has significance across the entire KMI (i.e., the identity's registration data is maintained in a database at the PRSN level of the system, rather than only at an MGC) and for which a product can be generated and wrapped by a PSN for distribution to the specific device.
KOA Agent	A user identity that is designated by a KOA manager to access PRSN product delivery enclaves for the purpose of retrieving wrapped products that have been ordered for user devices that are assigned to that KOA.
KOA Manager	The Management Role that is responsible for the operation of one or KOA's (i.e., manages distribution of KMI products to the end cryptographic units, fill devices, and ADPs that are assigned to the manager's KOA).
KOA Registration Manager	The individual responsible for performing activities related to registering KOAs.

L

label	See Security Label.
labeled security protections	Access control protection features of a system that use security labels to make access control decisions.

laboratory attack (C.F.D.)	Use of sophisticated signal recovery equipment in a laboratory environment to recover information from data storage media.
least privilege	The principle that a security architecture should be designed so that each entity is granted the minimum system resources and authorizations that the entity needs to perform its function.
least trust	The principal that a security architecture should be designed in a way that minimizes 1) the number of components that require trust and 2) the extent to which each component is trusted.
Level of Concern (C.F.D.)	Rating assigned to an information system indicating the extent to which protection measures, techniques, and procedures must be applied. High, Medium, and Basic are identified levels of concern. A separate Level-of-Concern is assigned to each information system for confidentiality, integrity, and availability.
Level of Protection (C.F.D.)	Extent to which protective measures, techniques, and procedures must be applied to information systems and networks based on risk, threat, vulnerability, system interconnectivity considerations, and Information Assurance needs. Levels of protection are: 1) Basic - information systems and networks requiring implementation of standard minimum security countermeasures. 2) Medium - information systems and networks requiring layering of additional safeguards above the standard minimum security countermeasures. 3) High - information systems and networks requiring the most stringent protection and rigorous security countermeasures.
likelihood of occurrence	In Information Assurance risk analysis, a weighted factor based on a subjective analysis of the probability that a given threat is capable of exploiting a given vulnerability.
limited maintenance (C.F.D.)	COMSEC maintenance restricted to fault isolation, removal, and replacement of plug-in assemblies. Soldering or unsoldering usually is prohibited in limited maintenance. See full maintenance.
line conditioning	Elimination of unintentional signals or noise induced or conducted on a telecommunications or information system signal, power, control, indicator, or other external interface line.
line conduction	Unintentional signals or noise induced or conducted on a telecommunications or information system signal, power, control, indicator, or other external interface line.
link encryption	Encryption of information between nodes of a communications system.
list-oriented (C.F.D.)	Information system protection in which each protected object has a list of all subjects authorized to access it.
local access	Access to an organizational information system by a user (or process acting on behalf of a user) communicating through a direct connection without the use of a network.

local authority	Organization responsible for generating and signing user certificates in a PKI-enabled environment.
Local Management Device/ Key Processor (LMD/KP)	EKMS platform providing automated management of COMSEC material and generating key for designated users.
Local Registration Authority (LRA)	A Registration Authority with responsibility for a local community in a PKI-enabled environment.
logic bomb	A piece of code intentionally inserted into a software system that will set off a malicious function when specified conditions are met.
logical completeness measure (C.F.D.)	Means for assessing the effectiveness and degree to which a set of security and access control mechanisms meets security specifications.
logical perimeter	A conceptual perimeter that extends to all intended users of the system, both directly and indirectly connected, who receive output from the system. without a reliable human review by an appropriate authority. The location of such a review is commonly referred to as an "air gap."
long title	Descriptive title of a COMSEC item.
low impact	The loss of confidentiality, integrity, or availability that could be expected to have a limited adverse effect on organizational operations, organizational assets, individuals, other organizations, or the national security interests of the United States; (i.e., 1) causes a degradation in mission capability to an extent and duration that the organization is able to perform its primary functions, but the effectiveness of the functions is noticeably reduced; 2) results in minor damage to organizational assets; 3) results in minor financial loss; or 4) results in minor harm to individuals.
low probability of detection (LPD)	Result of measures used to hide or disguise intentional electromagnetic transmissions.
low probability of intercept (LPI)	Result of measures to prevent the capture of intentional electromagnetic transmissions. The objective is to minimize an adversary's capability of receiving processing, or replaying an electronic signal.
low-impact system	An information system in which all three security properties (i.e., confidentiality, integrity, and availability) are assigned a potential impact value of low.

M

macro virus	A virus that attaches itself to documents and uses the macro programming capabilities of the document's application to execute and propagate.
magnetic remanence	Magnetic representation of residual information remaining on a magnetic medium after the medium has been cleared. See clearing.

maintenance hook (C.F.D.)	Special instructions (trapdoors) in software allowing easy maintenance and additional feature development. Since maintenance hooks frequently allow entry into the code without the usual checks, they are a serious security risk if they are not removed prior to live implementation.
maintenance key	Key intended only for in-shop use.
malicious applets	Small application programs that are automatically downloaded and executed and that perform an unauthorized function on an information system.
malicious code	Software or firmware intended to perform an unauthorized process that will have adverse impact on the confidentiality, integrity, or availability of an information system. A virus, worm, Trojan horse, or other code-based entity that infects a host. Spyware and some forms of adware are also examples of malicious code.
malicious logic	Hardware, firmware, or software that is intentionally included or inserted in a system for a harmful purpose.
malware	See malicious code, malicious applets, and malicious logic.
Management Client (MGC)	A configuration of a client node that enables a KMI external operational manager to manage KMI products and services by either 1) accessing a PRSN or 2) exercising locally-provided capabilities. An MGC consists of a client platform and an advanced key processor (AKP).
	NIST SP 800-53: The security controls (i.e., safeguards or countermeasures) for an information system that focus on the management of risk and the management of information system security.
management controls	Actions taken to manage the development, maintenance, and use of the system, including system-specific policies, procedures and rules of behavior, individual roles and responsibilities, individual accountability, and personnel security decisions.
management security controls	The security controls (i.e., safeguards or countermeasures) for an information system that focus on the management of risk and the management of information systems security.
Mandatory Access Control (MAC)	A means of restricting access to objects based on the sensitivity (as represented by a security label) of the information contained in the objects and the formal authorization (i.e., clearance, formal access approvals, and need-to-know) of subjects to access information of such sensitivity.
mandatory modification	Change to a COMSEC end-item that NSA requires to be completed and reported by a specified date. See optional modification.
Man-in-the-Middle Attack (MitM)	A form of active wiretapping attack in which the attacker intercepts and selectively modifies communicated data to masquerade as one or more of the entities involved in a communication association.

manipulative communications deception (C.F.D.)	Alteration or simulation of friendly telecommunications for the purpose of deception. See communications deception and imitative communications deception.
manual cryptosystem	Cryptosystem in which the cryptographic processes are performed without the use of crypto-equipment or auto-manual devices.
manual remote rekeying	Procedure by which a distant crypto-equipment is rekeyed electronically, with specific actions required by the receiving terminal operator. Synonymous with cooperative remote rekeying. See also automatic remote keying.
marking	See security markings.
masquerading	A type of threat action whereby an unauthorized entity gains access to a system or performs a malicious act by illegitimately posing as an authorized entity.
master cryptographic ignition key (C.F.D.)	Key device with electronic logic and circuits providing the capability for adding more operational CIKs to a keyset.
match/matching	The process of comparing biometric information against a previously stored template(s) and scoring the level of similarity.
media	Physical devices or writing surfaces including but not limited to magnetic tapes, optical disks, magnetic disks, LSI memory chips, printouts (but not including display media) onto which information is recorded, stored, or printed within an information system.
media sanitization	The actions taken to render data written on media unrecoverable by both ordinary and extraordinary means.
Memorandum of Understanding/Agreement (MOU/A)	A document established between two or more parties to define their respective responsibilities in accomplishing a particular goal or mission, e.g., establishing, operating, and securing a system interconnection.
memory scavenging	The collection of residual information from data storage.
message authentication code	See checksum.
Message Authentication Code (MAC)	A specific ANSI standard for a checksum.
message digest	A cryptographic checksum typically generated for a file that can be used to detect changes to the file. Synonymous with hash value/result.
message externals (C.F.D.)	Information outside of the message text, such as the header, trailer, etc.
message indicator	Sequence of bits transmitted over a communications system for synchronizing cryptographic equipment.
mimicking (C.F.D.)	See spoofing.

misnamed files	A technique used to disguise a file's content (e.g., password file) by changing the file's name to something innocuous or altering its extension to a different type of file, forcing the examiner to identify the files by file signature versus file extension.
Mission Assurance Category (MAC) (*L)	A Department of Defense Information Assurance Certification and Accreditation Process (DIACAP) term primarily used to determine the requirements for availability and integrity.
mobile code	Software programs or parts of programs obtained from remote information systems, transmitted across a network, and executed on a local information system without explicit installation or execution by the recipient. Note: Some examples of software technologies that provide the mechanisms for the production and use of mobile code include Java, JavaScript, ActiveX, VBScript, etc.
Mode of Operation (C.F.D.)	Description of the conditions under which an information system operates based on the sensitivity of information processed and the clearance levels, formal access approvals, and need-to-know of its users. Four modes of operation are authorized for processing or transmitting information: dedicated mode, system high mode, compartmented/partitioned mode, and multilevel mode.
moderate impact	The loss of confidentiality, integrity, or availability that could be expected to have a serious adverse effect on organizational operations, organizational assets, individuals, other organizations, or the national security interests of the United States; (i.e., 1) causes a significant degradation in mission capability to an extent and duration that the organization is able to perform its primary functions, but the effectiveness of the functions is significantly reduced; 2) results in significant damage to organizational assets; 3) results in significant financial loss; or 4) results in significant harm to individuals that does not involve loss of life or serious life threatening injuries.).
moderate impact system	An information system in which at least one security objective (i.e., confidentiality, integrity, or availability) is assigned a potential impact value of moderate and no security objective is assigned a potential impact value of high.
multilevel device	Equipment trusted to properly maintain and separate data of different security domains.
multilevel mode (C.F.D.)	Mode of operation wherein all the following statements are satisfied concerning the users who have direct or indirect access to the system, its peripherals, remote terminals, or remote hosts: 1) some users do not have a valid security clearance for all the information processed in the information system; 2) all users have the proper security clearance and appropriate formal access approval for that information to which they have access; and 3) all users have a valid need-to-know only for information to which they have access.
Multilevel Security (MLS)	Concept of processing information with different classifications and categories that simultaneously permits access by users with different security clearances and denies access to users who lack authorization.

Multiple Security Levels (MSL)	Capability of an information system that is trusted to contain, and maintain separation between, resources (particularly stored data) of different security domains.
multi-releasable	A characteristic of an information domain where access control mechanisms enforce policy-based release of information to authorized users within the information domain.
mutual authentication	The process of both entities involved in a transaction verifying each other.
mutual suspicion (C.F.D.)	Condition in which two information systems need to rely upon each other to perform a service, yet neither trusts the other to properly protect shared data.

N

National Information Assurance Partnership (NIAP)	A U.S. Government initiative established to promote the use of evaluated information systems products and champion the development and use of national and international standards for information technology security. NIAP was originally established as collaboration between the National Institute of Standards and Technology (NIST) and the National Security Agency (NSA) in fulfilling their respective responsibilities under P.L. 100-235 (Computer Security Act of 1987). NIST officially withdrew from the partnership in 2007 but NSA continues to manage and operate the program. The key operational component of NIAP is the Common Criteria Evaluation and Validation Scheme (CCEVS) which is the only U.S. Government-sponsored and endorsed program for conducting internationally-recognized security evaluations of commercial off-the-shelf (COTS) Information Assurance (IA) and IA-enabled information technology products. NIAP employs the CCEVS to provide government oversight or "validation" to U.S. CC evaluations to ensure correct conformance to the International Common Criteria for IT Security Evaluation (ISO/IEC 15408).
National Information Infrastructure (NII)	Nationwide interconnection of communications networks, computers, databases, and consumer electronics that make vast amounts of information available to users. It includes both public and private networks, the internet, the public switched network, and cable, wireless, and satellite communications.
National Security Emergency Preparedness Telecommunications Services	Telecommunications services that are used to maintain a state of readiness or to respond to and manage any event or crisis (local, national, or international) that causes or could cause injury or harm to the population, damage to or loss of property, or degrade or threaten the national security or emergency preparedness posture of the United States.
National Security Information (NSI)	See classified nation security information.

National Security System (NSS)	Any information system (including any telecommunications system) used or operated by an agency or by a contractor of an agency, or other organization on behalf of an agency--
	      (i) the function, operation, or use of which--
	         (I) involves intelligence activities;
	         (II) involves cryptologic activities related to national security;
	         (III) involves command and control of military forces;
	         (IV) involves equipment that is an integral part of a weapon or weapons system; or
	         (V) subject to subparagraph (B), is critical to the direct fulfillment of military or intelligence missions; or
	
	      (ii) is protected at all times by procedures established for information that have been specifically authorized under criteria established by an Executive order or an Act of Congress to be kept classified in the interest of national defense or foreign policy.
	
	      (B) Subparagraph (A)(i)(V) does not include a system that is to be used for routine administrative and business applications (including payroll, finance, logistics, and personnel management applications). [44 U.S.C. 3542(b)(2)]

National Vulnerability Database (NVD)	The U.S. Government repository of standards based vulnerability management data, enabling automation of vulnerability management, security measurement, and compliance (e.g., FISMA).
need-to-know	A method of isolating information resources based on a user's need to have access to that resource in order to perform their job but no more. The terms 'need-to know" and "least privilege" express the same idea. Need-to-know is generally applied to people, while least privilege is generally applied to processes.
need-to-know determination	Decision made by an authorized holder of official information that a prospective recipient requires access to specific official information to carry out official duties.
network	Information system(s) implemented with a collection of interconnected components. Such components may include routers, hubs, cabling, telecommunications controllers, key distribution centers, and technical control devices.
network access	Access to an organizational information system by a user (or a process acting on behalf of a user) communicating through a network (e.g., local area network, wide area network, Internet).
network front-end (C.F.D.)	Device implementing protocols that allow attachment of a computer system to a network.
network reference monitor (C.F.D.)	See reference monitor.

network resilience	A computing infrastructure that provides continuous business operation (i.e., highly resistant to disruption and able to operate in a degraded mode if damaged), rapid recovery if failure does occur, and the ability to scale to meet rapid or unpredictable demands.
network security (C.F.D.)	See Information Assurance.
network security officer (C.F.D.)	See information systems security officer and information assurance officer.
network sponsor (C.F.D.)	Individual or organization responsible for stating the security policy enforced by the network, designing the network security architecture to properly enforce that policy, and ensuring the network is implemented in such a way that the policy is enforced.
network system (C.F.D.)	System implemented with a collection of interconnected components. A network system is based on a coherent security architecture and design.
network weaving (C.F.D.)	Penetration technique in which different communication networks are linked to access an information system to avoid detection and trace-back.
No-Lone Zone (NLZ)	Area, room, or space that, when staffed, must be occupied by two or more appropriately cleared individuals who remain within sight of each other. See two-person integrity.
nonce	A random or non-repeating value that is included in data exchanged by a protocol, usually for the purpose of guaranteeing the transmittal of live data rather than replayed data, thus detecting and protecting against replay attacks.
non-repudiation	Assurance that the sender of information is provided with proof of delivery and the recipient is provided with proof of the sender's identity, so neither can later deny having processed the information. NIST 800-53: Protection against an individual falsely denying having performed a particular action. Provides the capability to determine whether a given individual took a particular action such as creating information, sending a message, approving information, and receiving a message.
null	Dummy letter, letter symbol, or code group inserted into an encrypted message to delay or prevent its decryption or to complete encrypted groups for transmission or transmission security purposes.

O

object	Passive information system-related entity (e.g., devices, files, records, tables, processes, programs, domains) containing or receiving information. Access to an object implies access to the information it contains.
object reuse	Reassignment and reuse of a storage medium containing one or more objects after ensuring no residual data remains on the storage medium.

official information (C.F.D.)	All information in the custody and control of a U.S. Government department or agency that was acquired by U.S. Government employees as a part of their official duties or because of their official status and has not been cleared for public release.
off-line cryptosystem	Cryptographic system in which encryption and decryption are performed independently of the transmission and reception functions.
one-part code	Code in which plain text elements and their accompanying code groups are arranged in alphabetical, numerical, or other systematic order, so one listing serves for both encoding and decoding. One-part codes are normally small codes used to pass small volumes of low-sensitivity information.
one-time cryptosystem	Cryptosystem employing key used only once.
one-time pad	Manual one-time cryptosystem produced in pad form.
one-time tape	Punched paper tape used to provide key streams on a one-time basis in certain machine cryptosystems.
one-way hash algorithm	Hash algorithms which map arbitrarily long inputs into a fixed-size output such that it is very difficult (computationally infeasible) to find two different hash inputs that produce the same output. Such algorithms are an essential part of the process of producing fixed-size digital signatures that can both authenticate the signer and provide for data integrity checking (detection of input modification after signature).
on-line cryptosystem	Cryptographic system in which encryption and decryption are performed in association with the transmitting and receiving functions.
open storage	Any storage of classified national security information outside of approved containers. This includes classified information that is resident on information systems media and outside of an approved storage container, regardless of whether or not that media is in use (i.e., unattended operations).
operational controls	The security controls (i.e., safeguards or countermeasures) for an information system that are primarily implemented and executed by people (as opposed to systems).
operational key	Key intended for use over-the-air for protection of operational information or for the production or secure electrical transmission of key streams.
operational vulnerability information (C.F.D.)	Information that describes the presence of an information vulnerability within a specific operational setting or network.
operational waiver	Authority for continued use of unmodified COMSEC end-items pending the completion of a mandatory modification.
operations code	Code composed largely of words and phrases suitable for general communications use.

Operations Security (OPSEC)	Systematic and proven process by which potential adversaries can be denied information about capabilities and intentions by identifying, controlling, and protecting generally unclassified evidence of the planning and execution of sensitive activities. The process involves five steps: identification of critical information, analysis of threats, analysis of vulnerabilities, assessment of risks, and application of appropriate countermeasures.
optional modification	NSA-approved modification not required for universal implementation by all holders of a COMSEC end-item. This class of modification requires all of the engineering/doctrinal control of mandatory modification but is usually not related to security, safety, TEMPEST, or reliability. See mandatory modification.
organizational maintenance (C.F.D.)	Limited maintenance performed by a user organization.
Organizational Registration Authority (ORA)	Entity within the PKI that authenticates the identity and the organizational affiliation of the users.
outside(r) threat	An unauthorized entity outside the security domain that has the potential to harm an information system through destruction, disclosure, modification of data, and/or denial of service.
overt channel	Communications path within a computer system or network designed for the authorized transfer of data. See covert channel.
Over-The-Air Key Distribution (OTAD)	Providing electronic key via over-the-air rekeying, over-the-air key transfer, or cooperative key generation.
Over-The-Air Key Transfer (OTAT)	Electronically distributing key without changing traffic encryption key used on the secured communications path over which the transfer is accomplished.
Over-The-Air Rekeying (OTAR)	Changing traffic encryption key or transmission security key in remote cryptographic equipment by sending new key directly to the remote cryptographic equipment over the communications path it secures.
overwrite procedure	A software process that replaces data previously stored on storage media with a predetermined set of meaningless data or random patterns.

P

packet sniffer	Software that observes and records network traffic.
parity	Bit(s) used to determine whether a block of data has been altered.
partitioned security mode (C.F.D.)	Information systems security mode of operation wherein all personnel have the clearance, but not necessarily formal access approval and need-to-know, for all information handled by an information system.
passive attack	An attack that does not alter systems or data.
passive wiretapping	The monitoring or recording of data while it is being transmitted over a communications link, without altering or affecting the data.

password (C.F.D.)	A protected/private string of letters, numbers, and/or special characters used to authenticate an identity or to authorize access to data.
patch management	The systematic notification, identification, deployment, installation, and verification of operating system and application software code revisions. These revisions are known as patches, hot fixes, and service packs.
peer entity authentication	The process of verifying that a peer entity in an association is as claimed.
penetration	See intrusion.
penetration testing	A test methodology in which assessors, typically working under specific constraints, attempt to circumvent or defeat the security features of an information system.
per-call key	Unique traffic encryption key generated automatically by certain secure telecommunications systems to secure single voice or data transmissions. See cooperative key generation.
performance reference model (PRM)	Framework for performance measurement providing common output measurements throughout the Federal Government. It allows agencies to better manage the business of government at a strategic level by providing a means for using an agency's EA to measure the success of information systems investments and their impact on strategic outcomes.
perimeter	(*L) Encompasses all those components of the system that are to be accredited by the DAA, and excludes separately accredited systems to which the system is connected.
	(*T) Encompasses all those components of the system or network for which a Body of Evidence is provided in support of a formal approval to operate.
periods processing	The processing of various levels of classified and unclassified information at distinctly different times. Under the concept of periods processing, the system must be purged of all information from one processing period before transitioning to the next.
perishable data	Information whose value can decrease substantially during a specified time. A significant decrease in value occurs when the operational circumstances change to the extent that the information is no longer useful.
permuter (C.F.D.)	Device used in cryptographic equipment to change the order in which the contents of a shift register are used in various nonlinear combining circuits.
Personal Identification Number (PIN)	A short numeric code used to confirm identity.
Personal Identity Verification (PIV)	The process of creating and using a government-wide secure and reliable form of identification for Federal employees and contractors, in support of HSPD 12, *Policy for a Common Identification Standard for Federal Employees and Contractors*.

Personal Identity Verification (PIV) Authorizing Official	An individual who can act on behalf of an agency to authorize the issuance of a credential to an applicant.
Personal Identity Verification (PIV) card	Physical artifact (e.g., identity card, "smart" card) issued to an individual that contains stored identity credentials (e.g., photograph, cryptographic keys, digitized fingerprint representation etc.) such that a claimed identity of the cardholder may be verified against the stored credentials by another person (human readable and verifiable) or an automated process (computer readable and verifiable).
Personal Identity Verification Accreditation	The official management decision to authorize operation of a PIV Card Issuer after determining that the Issuer's reliability has satisfactorily been established through appropriate assessment and certification processes.
Personally Identifiable Information (PII)	Information which can be used to distinguish or trace an individual's identity, such as their name, social security number, biometric records, etc. alone, or when combined with other personal or identifying information which is linked or linkable to a specific individual, such as date and place of birth, mother's maiden name, etc.
personnel registration manager	The management role that is responsible for registering human users, i.e., users that are people.
phishing	Deceiving individuals into disclosing sensitive personal information through deceptive computer-based means.
plaintext	Unencrypted information.
Plan of Action and Milestones (POA&M)	A document that identifies tasks needing to be accomplished. It details resources required to accomplish the elements of the plan, any milestones in meeting the tasks, and scheduled completion dates for the milestones.
Policy Approving Authority (PAA) (C.F.D.)	First level of the PKI Certification Management Authority that approves the security policy of each PCA.
Policy Based Access Control (PBAC)	A form of access control that uses an authorization policy that is flexible in the types of evaluated parameters (e.g., identity, role, clearance, operational need, risk, heuristics).
Policy Certification Authority (PCA) (C.F.D.)	Second level of the PKI Certification Management Authority that formulates the security policy under which it and its subordinate CAs will issue public key certificates.
port scanning	Using a program to remotely determine which ports on a system are open (e.g., whether systems allow connections through those ports).
Portable Electronic Device (PED)	Any non-stationary electronic apparatus with singular or multiple capabilities of recording, storing, and/or transmitting data, voice, video, or photo images. This includes but is not limited to laptops, personal digital assistants, pocket personal computers, palmtops, MP3 players, cellular telephones, video cameras, and pagers.

positive control material	Generic term referring to a sealed authenticator system, permissive action link, coded switch system, positive enable system, or nuclear command and control documents, material, or devices.
potential impact	The loss of confidentiality, integrity, or availability that could be expected to have a limited (low) adverse effect, a serious (moderate) adverse effect, or a severe or catastrophic (high) adverse effect on organizational operations, organizational assets, or individuals.
precursor	A sign that an attacker may be preparing to cause an incident. See indicator.
preproduction model (C.F.D.)	Version of INFOSEC equipment employing standard parts and suitable for complete evaluation of form, design, and performance. Preproduction models are often referred to as beta models.
Primary Services Node (PRSN)	A Key Management Infrastructure core node that provides the users' central point of access to KMI products, services, and information.
Principal Accrediting Authority (PAA) (*L)	Senior official with authority and responsibility for all intelligence systems within an agency.
print suppression (C.F.D.)	Eliminating the display of characters in order to preserve their secrecy.
Privacy Impact Assessment (PIA)	An analysis of how information is handled 1) to ensure handling conforms to applicable legal, regulatory, and policy requirements regarding privacy; 2) to determine the risks and effects of collecting, maintaining, and disseminating information in identifiable form in an electronic information system; and 3) to examine and evaluate protections and alternative processes for handling information to mitigate potential privacy risks.
privacy system (C.F.D.)	Commercial encryption system that affords telecommunications limited protection to deter a casual listener, but cannot withstand a technically competent cryptanalytic attack.
private key	In an asymmetric cryptography scheme, the private or secret key of a key pair which must be kept confidential and is used to decrypt messages encrypted with the public key or to digitally sign messages, which can then be validated with the public key.
privilege	A right granted to an individual, a program, or a process.
privileged account	An information system account with approved authorizations of a privileged user.
privileged command	A human-initiated command executed on an information system involving the control, monitoring, or administration of the system including security functions and associated security-relevant information.
privileged process	A computer process that is authorized (and, therefore, trusted) to perform security-relevant functions that ordinary processes are not authorized to perform.

privileged user	A user that is authorized (and, therefore, trusted) to perform security-relevant functions that ordinary users are not authorized to perform.
probability of occurrence	See likelihood of occurrence.
probe	A technique that attempts to access a system to learn something about the system.
Product Source Node (PSN)	The Key Management Infrastructure core node that provides central generation of cryptographic key material.
production model (C.F.D.)	INFOSEC equipment in its final mechanical and electrical form.
profiling	Measuring the characteristics of expected activity so that changes to it can be more easily identified.
proprietary information (PROPIN)	Material and information relating to or associated with a company's products, business, or activities, including but not limited to financial information; data or statements; trade secrets; product research and development; existing and future product designs and performance specifications; marketing plans or techniques; schematics; client lists; computer programs; processes; and know-how that has been clearly identified and properly marked by the company as proprietary information, trade secrets, or company confidential information. The information must have been developed by the company and not be available to the Government or to the public without restriction from another source.
Protected Distribution System (PDS)	Wire line or fiber optic system that includes adequate safeguards and/or countermeasures (e.g., acoustic, electric, electromagnetic, and physical) to permit its use for the transmission of unencrypted information through an area of lesser classification or control.
protection philosophy	Informal description of the overall design of an information system delineating each of the protection mechanisms employed. Combination of formal and informal techniques, appropriate to the evaluation class, used to show the mechanisms are adequate to enforce the security policy.
protection profile	Common Criteria specification that represents an implementation-independent set of security requirements for a category of Target of Evaluations (TOE) that meets specific consumer needs.
protective packaging	Packaging techniques for COMSEC material that discourage penetration, reveal a penetration has occurred or was attempted, or inhibit viewing or copying of keying material prior to the time it is exposed for use.
protective technologies	Special tamper-evident features and materials employed for the purpose of detecting tampering and deterring attempts to compromise, modify, penetrate, extract, or substitute information processing equipment and keying material.
protocol	Set of rules and formats, semantic and syntactic, permitting information systems to exchange information.

| proxy | An application that "breaks" the connection between client and server. The proxy accepts certain types of traffic entering or leaving a network and processes it and forwards it.

Note: This effectively closes the straight path between the internal and external networks making it more difficult for an attacker to obtain internal addresses and other details of the organization's internal network. Proxy servers are available for common Internet services; for example, a Hyper Text Transfer Protocol (HTTP) proxy used for Web access, and a Simple Mail Transfer Protocol (SMTP) proxy used for e-mail. |

| proxy agent | A software application running on a firewall or on a dedicated proxy server that is capable of filtering a protocol and routing it between the interfaces of the device. |

| proxy server | A server that services the requests of its clients by forwarding those requests to other servers. |

| Pseudo Random Number Generator (PRNG) | An algorithm that produces a sequence of bits that are uniquely determined from an initial value called a seed. The output of the PRNG "appears" to be random, i.e., the output is statistically indistinguishable from random values. A cryptographic PRNG has the additional property that the output is unpredictable, given that the seed is not known. |

| pseudonym | 1. A subscriber name that has been chosen by the subscriber that is not verified as meaningful by identity proofing.

2. An assigned identity that is used to protect an individual's true identity. |

| public domain software | Software not protected by copyright laws of any nation that may be freely used without permission of, or payment to, the creator, and that carries no warranties from, or liabilities to the creator. |

| public key | A cryptographic key that may be widely published and is used to enable the operation of an asymmetric cryptography scheme. This key is mathematically linked with a corresponding private key. Typically, a public key can be used to encrypt, but not decrypt, or to validate a signature, but not to sign. |

| public key certificate | See certificate. |

| Public Key Cryptography (PKC) | Encryption system that uses a public-private key pair for encryption and/or digital signature. |

| Public Key Enabling (PKE) | The incorporation of the use of certificates for security services such as authentication, confidentiality, data integrity, and non-repudiation. |

Public Key Infrastructure (PKI)	The framework and services that provide for the generation, production, distribution, control, accounting and destruction of public key certificates. Components include the personnel, policies, processes, server platforms, software, and workstations used for the purpose of administering certificates and public-private key pairs, including the ability to issue, maintain, recover, and revoke public key certificates.
public seed	A starting value for a pseudorandom number generator. The value produced by the random number generator may be made public. The public seed is often called a "salt."
purge	Rendering sanitized data unrecoverable by laboratory attack methods.

Q

quadrant	Short name referring to technology that provides tamper-resistant protection to cryptographic equipment.
Quality of Service	The measurable end-to-end performance properties of a network service, which can be guaranteed in advance by a Service Level Agreement between a user and a service provider, so as to satisfy specific customer application requirements. Note: These properties may include throughput (bandwidth), transit delay (latency), error rates, priority, security, packet loss, packet jitter, etc.

R

Random Number Generator (RNG)	A process used to generate an unpredictable series of numbers. Each individual value is called random if each of the values in the total population of values has an equal probability of being selected.
randomizer	Analog or digital source of unpredictable, unbiased, and usually independent bits. Randomizers can be used for several different functions, including key generation or to provide a starting state for a key generator.
read (C.F.D.)	Fundamental operation in an information system that results only in the flow of information from an object to a subject.
read access (C.F.D.)	Permission to read information in an information system.
real time reaction	Immediate response to a penetration attempt that is detected and diagnosed in time to prevent access.
reciprocity	Mutual agreement among participating enterprises to accept each other's security assessments in order to reuse information system resources and/or to accept each other's assessed security posture in order to share information.

records	The recordings (automated and/or manual) of evidence of activities performed or results achieved (e.g., forms, reports, test results), which serve as a basis for verifying that the organization and the information system are performing as intended. Also used to refer to units of related data fields (i.e., groups of data fields that can be accessed by a program and that contain the complete set of information on particular items).
records management	The process for tagging information for records keeping requirements as mandated in the Federal Records Act and the National Archival and Records Requirements.
recovery procedures	Actions necessary to restore data files of an information system and computational capability after a system failure.
RED	In cryptographic systems, refers to information or messages that contain sensitive or classified information that is not encrypted. See also BLACK.
Red signal	Any electronic emission (e.g., plain text, key, key stream, subkey stream, initial fill, or control signal) that would divulge national security information if recovered.
Red Team	A group of people authorized and organized to emulate a potential adversary's attack or exploitation capabilities against an enterprise's security posture. The Red Team's objective is to improve enterprise Information Assurance by demonstrating the impacts of successful attacks and by demonstrating what works for the defenders (i.e., the Blue Team) in an operational environment.
Red/Black concept	Separation of electrical and electronic circuits, components, equipment, and systems that handle unencrypted information (Red), in electrical form, from those that handle encrypted information (Black) in the same form.
reference monitor (C.F.D.)	Concept of an abstract machine that enforces Target of Evaluation (TOE) access control policies.
registration	The process through which a party applies to become a subscriber of a Credentials Service Provider (CSP) and a Registration Authority validates the identity of that party on behalf of the CSP.
Registration Authority (RA)	A trusted entity that establishes and vouches for the identity of a subscriber to a Credentials Service Provider (CSP). The RA may be an integral part of a CSP, or it may be independent of a CSP, but it has a relationship to the CSP(s).
re-key	To change the value of a cryptographic key that is being used in a cryptographic system/application.
release prefix	Prefix appended to the short title of U.S.-produced keying material to indicate its foreign releasability. "A" designates material that is releasable to specific allied nations and "U.S." designates material intended exclusively for U. S. use.

relying party	An entity that relies upon the subscriber's credentials, typically to process a transaction or grant access to information or a system.
remanence	Residual information remaining on storage media after clearing. See magnetic remanence and clearing.
remediation	The act of mitigating a vulnerability or a threat.
remote access	Access to an organization's nonpublic information system by an authorized user (or an information system) communicating through an external, non-organization-controlled network (e.g., the Internet). NIST 800-53: Access to an organizational information system by a user (or a process acting on behalf of a user) communicating through an external network (e.g., the Internet).
remote diagnostics/maintenance	Maintenance activities conducted by authorized individuals communicating through an external network (e.g., the Internet).
remote rekeying	Procedure by which a distant crypto-equipment is rekeyed electrically. See automatic remote rekeying and manual remote rekeying.
removable media	Portable electronic storage media such as magnetic, optical, and solid state devices, which can be inserted into and removed from a computing device, and that is used to store text, video, audio, and image information. Such devices have no independent processing capabilities. Examples include hard disks, floppy disks, zip drives, compact disks (CD), thumb drives, pen drives, and similar USB storage devices.
repair action (C.F.D.)	NSA-approved change to a COMSEC end-item that does not affect the original characteristics of the end-item and is provided for optional application by holders. Repair actions are limited to minor electrical and/or mechanical improvements to enhance operation, maintenance, or reliability. They do not require an identification label, marking, or control but must be fully documented by changes to the maintenance manual.
replay attacks	An attack that involves the capture of transmitted authentication or access control information and its subsequent retransmission with the intent of producing an unauthorized effect or gaining unauthorized access.
reserve keying material	Key held to satisfy unplanned needs. See contingency key.
residual risk	Portion of risk remaining after security measures have been applied.
residue	Data left in storage after information processing operations are complete, but before degaussing or overwriting has taken place.
resource encapsulation (C.F.D.)	Method by which the reference monitor mediates accesses to an information system resource. Resource is protected and not directly accessible by a subject. Satisfies requirement for accurate auditing of resource usage.

responsibility to provide	An information distribution approach whereby relevant essential information is made readily available and discoverable to the broadest possible pool of potential users.

risk

A measure of the extent to which an entity is threatened by a potential circumstance or event, and typically a function of 1) the adverse impacts that would arise if the circumstance or event occurs; and 2) the likelihood of occurrence.

Note: Information system-related security risks are those risks that arise from the loss of confidentiality, integrity, or availability of information or information systems and reflect the potential adverse impacts to organizational operations (including mission, functions, image, or reputation), organizational assets, individuals, other organizations, and the Nation.

Risk Adaptable Access Control (RAdAC)

A form of access control that uses an authorization policy that takes into account operational need, risk, and heuristics.

risk analysis (C.F.D.)

Examination of information to identify the risk to an information system. See risk assessment.

risk assessment

The process of identifying, prioritizing, and estimating risks. This includes determining the extent to which adverse circumstances or events could impact an enterprise. Uses the results of threat and vulnerability assessments to identify risk to organizational operations and evaluates those risks in terms of likelihood of occurrence and impacts if they occur. The product of a risk assessment is a list of estimated, potential impacts and unmitigated vulnerabilities. Risk assessment is part of risk management and is conducted throughout the Risk Management Framework (RMF).

NIST SP 800-53: The process of identifying risks to organizational operations (including mission, functions, image, reputation), organizational assets, individuals, other organizations, and the Nation, resulting from the operation of an information system.

Part of risk management, incorporates threat and vulnerability analyses, and considers mitigations provided by security controls planned or in place. Synonymous with risk analysis.

risk executive (function)

An individual or group within an organization that helps to ensure that 1) security risk-related considerations for individual information systems, to include the authorization decisions for those systems, are viewed from an organization-wide perspective with regard to the overall strategic goals and objectives of the organization in carrying out its missions and business functions; and 2) managing risk from individual information systems is consistent across the organization, reflects organizational risk tolerance, and is considered along with other organizational risks affecting mission/business success.

risk management	The process of managing risks to organizational operations (including mission, functions, image, or reputation), organizational assets, individuals, other organizations, or the nation resulting from the operation or use of an information system, and includes: 1) the conduct of a risk assessment; 2) the implementation of a risk mitigation strategy; 3) employment of techniques and procedures for the continuous monitoring of the security state of the information system; and 4) documenting the overall risk management program. NIST SP 800-53: The process of managing risks to organizational operations (including mission, functions, image, or reputation), organizational assets, individuals, other organizations, or the Nation resulting from the operation of an information system, and includes: 1. the conduct of a risk assessment; 2. the implementation of a risk mitigation strategy; and 3. employment of techniques and procedures for the continuous monitoring of the security state of the information system.
Risk Management Framework (RMF)	A structured approach used to oversee and manage risk for an enterprise.
risk mitigation	Prioritizing, evaluating, and implementing the appropriate risk-reducing controls/countermeasures recommended from the risk management process.
risk tolerance	The defined impacts to an enterprise's information systems that an entity is willing to accept.
robustness	The ability of an Information Assurance entity to operate correctly and reliably across a wide range of operational conditions, and to fail gracefully outside of that operational range.
role	A group attribute that ties membership to function. When an entity assumes a role, the entity is given certain rights that belong to that role. When the entity leaves the role, those rights are removed. The rights given are consistent with the functionality that the entity needs to perform the expected tasks.
Role-Based Access Control (RBAC)	Access control based on user roles (i.e., a collection of access authorizations a user receives based on an explicit or implicit assumption of a given role). Role permissions may be inherited through a role hierarchy and typically reflect the permissions needed to perform defined functions within an organization. A given role may apply to a single individual or to several individuals.
Root Certification Authority	In a hierarchical Public Key Infrastructure, the Certification Authority whose public key serves as the most trusted datum (i.e., the beginning of trust paths) for a security domain.
rootkit	A set of tools used by an attacker after gaining root-level access to a host to conceal the attacker's activities on the host and permit the attacker to maintain root-level access to the host through covert means.
rule-based security policy	A security policy based on global rules imposed for all subjects. These rules usually rely on a comparison of the sensitivity of the objects being accessed and the possession of corresponding attributes by the subjects requesting access. Also known as discretionary access control (DAC).

ruleset	A table of instructions used by a controlled interface to determine what data is allowable and how the data is handled between interconnected systems.

S

safeguarding statement (C.F.D.)	Statement affixed to a computer output or printout that states the highest classification being processed at the time the product was produced and requires control of the product, at that level, until determination of the true classification by an authorized individual. Synonymous with banner.
safeguards	Protective measures prescribed to meet the security requirements (i.e., confidentiality, integrity, and availability) specified for an information system. Safeguards may include security features, management constraints, personnel security, and security of physical structures, areas, and devices. Synonymous with security controls and countermeasures.
salt	A non-secret value that is used in a cryptographic process, usually to ensure that the results of computations for one instance cannot be reused by an attacker.
sandboxing	A restricted, controlled execution environment that prevents potentially malicious software, such as mobile code, from accessing any system resources except those for which the software is authorized.
sanitization	A general term referring to the actions taken to render data written on media unrecoverable by both ordinary and, for some forms of sanitization, extraordinary means.
scanning	Sending packets or requests to another system to gain information to be used in a subsequent attack.
scavenging	Searching through object residue to acquire data.
scoping guidance	Specific factors related to technology, infrastructure, public access, scalability, common security controls, and risk that can be considered by organizations in the applicability and implementation of individual security controls in the security control baseline.

NIST SP 800-53: A part of tailoring guidance providing organizations with specific policy/regulatory-related, technology-related, system component allocation-related, operational/environmental-related, physical infrastructure-related, public access-related, scalability-related, common control-related, and security objective-related considerations on the applicability and implementation of individual security controls in the security control baseline. |
| secret key | A cryptographic key that is used with a symmetric cryptographic algorithm that is uniquely associated with one or more entities and is not made public. The use of the term "secret" in this context does not imply a classification level, but rather implies the need to protect the key from disclosure. |
| Secret Key (symmetric) Cryptographic Algorithm | A cryptographic algorithm that uses a single key (i.e., a secret key) for both encryption and decryption. |

secret seed	A secret value used to initialize a pseudorandom number generator.
secure communication protocol	A communication protocol that provides the appropriate confidentiality, authentication, and content integrity protection.
secure communications	Telecommunications deriving security through use of NSA-approved products and/or protected distribution systems (PDSs).
secure hash algorithm (SHA)	A hash algorithm with the property that is computationally infeasible 1) to find a message that corresponds to a given message digest, or 2) to find two different messages that produce the same message digest.
secure hash standard	Specification for a secure hash algorithm that can generate a condensed message representation called a message digest.
Secure Socket Layer (SSL)	A protocol used for protecting private information during transmission via the Internet. Note: SSL works by using a public key to encrypt data that's transferred over the SSL connection. Most web browsers support SSL and many web sites use the protocol to obtain confidential user information, such as credit card numbers. By convention, URLs that require an SSL connection start with "https:" instead of "http:."
secure state	Condition in which no subject can access any object in an unauthorized manner.
secure subsystem (C.F.D.)	Subsystem containing its own implementation of the reference monitor concept for those resources it controls. Secure subsystem must depend on other controls and the base operating system for the control of subjects and the more primitive system objects.
Secure/Multipurpose Internet Mail Extensions (S/MIME)	A set of specifications for securing electronic mail. Secure/ Multipurpose Internet Mail Extensions (S/MIME) is based upon the widely used MIME standard and describes a protocol for adding cryptographic security services through MIME encapsulation of digitally signed and encrypted objects. The basic security services offered by S/MIME are authentication, non-repudiation of origin, message integrity, and message privacy. Optional security services include signed receipts, security labels, secure mailing lists, and an extended method of identifying the signer's certificate(s).
security	A condition that results from the establishment and maintenance of protective measures that enable an enterprise to perform its mission or critical functions despite risks posed by threats to its use of information systems. Protective measures may involve a combination of deterrence, avoidance, prevention, detection, recovery, and correction that should form part of the enterprise's risk management approach.
Security Assertion Markup Language (SAML)	A protocol consisting of XML-based request and response message formats for exchanging security information, expressed in the form of assertions about subjects, between on-line business partners.

security association	A relationship established between two or more entities to enable them to protect data they exchange.
security attribute	An abstraction representing the basic properties or characteristics of an entity with respect to safeguarding information; typically associated with internal data structures (e.g., records, buffers, files) within the information system which are used to enable the implementation of access control and flow control policies; reflect special dissemination, handling, or distribution instructions; or support other aspects of the information security policy.
security authorization (to operate)	See authorization (to operate).
security banner	A banner at the top or bottom of a computer screen that states the overall classification of the system in large, bold type. Also can refer to the opening screen that informs users of the security implications of accessing a computer resource.
security category	The characterization of information or an information system based on an assessment of the potential impact that a loss of confidentiality, integrity, or availability of such information or information system would have on organizational operations, organizational assets, individuals, other organizations, and the Nation.
Security Concept of Operations (Security CONOP)	A security-focused description of an information system, its operational policies, classes of users, interactions between the system and its users, and the system's contribution to the operational mission.
Security Content Automation Protocol (SCAP)	A method for using specific standardized testing methods to enable automated vulnerability management, measurement, and policy compliance evaluation against a standardized set of security requirements.
security control assessment	The testing and/or evaluation of the management, operational, and technical security controls to determine the extent to which the controls are implemented correctly, operating as intended, and producing the desired outcome with respect to meeting the security requirements for the system or enterprise.
security control baseline	The set of minimum security controls defined for a low-impact, moderate-impact, or high-impact information system.
security control enhancements	Statements of security capability to 1) build in additional, but related, functionality to a basic control; and/or 2) increase the strength of a basic control.
security control inheritance	A situation in which an information system or application receives protection from security controls (or portions of security controls) that are developed, implemented, and assessed, authorized, and monitored by entities other than those responsible for the system or application; entities either internal or external to the organization where the system or application resides. See Common Control.
security controls	The management, operational, and technical controls (i.e., safeguards or countermeasures) prescribed for an information system to protect the confidentiality, integrity, and availability of the system and its information.

security domain	A domain that implements a security policy and is administered by a single authority.
security engineering	An interdisciplinary approach and means to enable the realization of secure systems. It focuses on defining customer needs, security protection requirements, and required functionality early in the systems development lifecycle, documenting requirements, and then proceeding with design, synthesis, and system validation while considering the complete problem.
Security Fault Analysis (SFA)	An assessment usually performed on information system hardware, to determine the security properties of a device when hardware fault is encountered.
Security Features Users Guide (SFUG)	Guide or manual explaining how the security mechanisms in a specific system work.
security filter	A secure subsystem of an information system that enforces security policy on the data passing through it.
security impact analysis	The analysis conducted by an organizational official to determine the extent to which changes to the information system have affected the security state of the system.
security incident	See incident.
security inspection	Examination of an information system to determine compliance with security policy, procedures, and practices.
security kernel	Hardware, firmware, and software elements of a trusted computing base implementing the reference monitor concept. Security kernel must mediate all accesses, be protected from modification, and be verifiable as correct.
security label	Information that represents or designates the value of one or more security relevant attributes (e.g., classification) of a system resource.
security marking	Human-readable indicators applied to a document, storage media, or hardware component to designate security classification, categorization and/or handling restrictions applicable to the information contained therein. For intelligence information, these could include compartment and sub-compartment indicators and handling restrictions.

NIST SP 800-53: Human-readable information affixed to information system components, removable media, or output indicating the distribution limitations, handling caveats and applicable security markings. |
| security mechanism | A device designed to provide one or more security services usually rated in terms of strength of service and assurance of the design. |
| security net control station (C.F.D.) | Management system overseeing and controlling implementation of network security policy. |

security perimeter	A physical or logical boundary that is defined for a system, domain, or enclave; within which a particular security policy or security architecture is applied.
security policy	A set of criteria for the provision of security services.
security posture	The security status of an enterprise's networks, information, and systems based on IA resources (e.g., people, hardware, software, policies) and capabilities in place to manage the defense of the enterprise and to react as the situation changes.
Security Program Plan	Formal document that provides an overview of the security requirements for an organization-wide information security program and describes the program management security controls and common security controls in place or planned for meeting those requirements.
security range	Highest and lowest security levels that are permitted in or on an information system, system component, subsystem, or network.
security relevant change	Any change to a system's configuration, environment, information content, functionality, or users which has the potential to change the risk imposed upon its continued operations.
security relevant event	An occurrence (e.g., an auditable event or flag) considered to have potential security implications to the system or its environment that may require further action (noting, investigating, or reacting).
security requirements	Requirements levied on an information system that are derived from applicable laws, Executive Orders, directives, policies, standards, instructions, regulations, or procedures, or organizational mission/business case needs to ensure the confidentiality, integrity, and availability of the information being processed, stored, or transmitted.
security requirements baseline	Description of the minimum requirements necessary for an information system to maintain an acceptable level of risk.
Security Requirements Traceability Matrix (SRTM)	Matrix that captures all security requirements linked to potential risks and addresses all applicable C&A requirements. It is, therefore, a correlation statement of a system's security features and compliance methods for each security requirement.
security safeguards	Protective measures and controls prescribed to meet the security requirements specified for an information system. Safeguards may include security features, management constraints, personnel security, and security of physical structures, areas, and devices.
security service	A capability that supports one, or more, of the security requirements (Confidentiality, Integrity, Availability). Examples of security services are key management, access control, and authentication.
security specification (C.F.D.)	Detailed description of the safeguards required to protect an information system.

security target	Common Criteria specification that represents a set of security requirements to be used as the basis of an evaluation of an identified Target of Evaluation (TOE).
Security Test and Evaluation (ST&E)	Examination and analysis of the safeguards required to protect an information system, as they have been applied in an operational environment, to determine the security posture of that system.
security testing (C.F.D.)	Process to determine that an information system protects data and maintains functionality as intended. See also security control assessment.
seed key	Initial key used to start an updating or key generation process.
Senior Agency Information Security Officer (SAISO)	Official responsible for carrying out the Chief Information Officer responsibilities under the Federal Information Security Management Act (FISMA) and serving as the Chief Information Officer's primary liaison to the agency's authorizing officials, information system owners, and information systems security officers. Note: Organizations subordinate to federal agencies may use the term Senior Information Security Officer or Chief Information Security Officer to denote individuals filling positions with similar responsibilities to Senior Agency Information Security Officers.
Sensitive Compartmented Information (SCI)	Classified information concerning or derived from intelligence sources, methods, or analytical processes, which is required to be handled within formal access control systems established by the Director of National Intelligence.
Sensitive Compartmented Information Facility (SCIF)	Accredited area, room, or group of rooms, buildings, or installation where SCI may be stored, used, discussed, and/or processed.
sensitive information (C.F.D.)	Information, the loss, misuse, or unauthorized access to or modification of, that could adversely affect the national interest or the conduct of federal programs, or the privacy to which individuals are entitled under 5 U.S.C. Section 552a (the Privacy Act), but that has not been specifically authorized under criteria established by an Executive Order or an Act of Congress to be kept classified in the interest of national defense or foreign policy. (Systems that are not national security systems, but contain sensitive information, are to be protected in accordance with the requirements of the Computer Security Act of 1987 (P.L.100-235).). See also controlled unclassified information.
sensitivity	A measure of the importance assigned to information by its owner, for the purpose of denoting its need for protection.
sensitivity label (C.F.D.)	Information representing elements of the security label(s) of a subject and an object. Sensitivity labels are used by the trusted computing base (TCB) as the basis for mandatory access control decisions. See security label.
service level agreement	Defines the specific responsibilities of the service provider and sets the customer expectations.

shielded enclosure	Room or container designed to attenuate electromagnetic radiation, acoustic signals, or emanations.
short title	Identifying combination of letters and numbers assigned to certain COMSEC materials to facilitate handling, accounting, and controlling.
signature	A recognizable, distinguishing pattern. See also attack signature or digital signature.
signature certificate	A public key certificate that contains a public key intended for verifying digital signatures rather than encrypting data or performing any other cryptographic functions.
single point keying	Means of distributing key to multiple, local crypto equipment or devices from a single fill point.
situational awareness	Within a volume of time and space, the perception of an enterprise's security posture and its threat environment; the comprehension/meaning of both taken together (risk); and the projection of their status into the near future.
smart card	A credit card-sized card with embedded integrated circuits that can store, process, and communicate information.
sniffer	See packet sniffer or passive wiretapping.
social engineering	An attempt to trick someone into revealing information (e.g., a password) that can be used to attack an enterprise.
software	Computer programs and associated data that may be dynamically written or modified during execution.
software assurance	Level of confidence that software is free from vulnerabilities, either intentionally designed into the software or accidentally inserted at anytime during its lifecycle and that the software functions in the intended manner.
software system test and evaluation process	Process that plans, develops, and documents the qualitative/quantitative demonstration of the fulfillment of all baseline functional performance, operational, and interface requirements.
spam	Electronic junk mail or the abuse of electronic messaging systems to indiscriminately send unsolicited bulk messages.
Special Access Program (SAP)	A program established for a specific class of classified information that imposes safeguarding and access requirements that exceed those normally required for information at the same classification level.
Special Access Program Facility (SAPF)	Facility formally accredited by an appropriate agency in accordance with DCID 6/9 in which SAP information may be processed.

special character	Any non-alphanumeric character that can be rendered on a standard, American-English keyboard. Use of a specific special character may be application dependent. The list of special characters follows.

` ~ ! @ # $ % ^ & * ( ) _ + | } { " : ? > < [ ] \ ; ' , . / - =

spillage	Security incident that results in the transfer of classified or CUI information onto an information system not accredited (i.e., authorized) for the appropriate security level.
split knowledge	1. Separation of data or information into two or more parts, each part constantly kept under control of separate authorized individuals or teams so that no one individual or team will know the whole data.

2. A process by which a cryptographic key is split into multiple key components, individually sharing no knowledge of the original key, which can be subsequently input into, or output from, a cryptographic module by separate entities and combined to recreate the original cryptographic key.

spoofing	1. Faking the sending address of a transmission to gain illegal entry into a secure system.

2. The deliberate inducement of a user or resource to take incorrect action.

Note: Impersonating, masquerading, piggybacking, and mimicking are forms of spoofing.

spread spectrum	Telecommunications techniques in which a signal is transmitted in a bandwidth considerably greater than the frequency content of the original information. Frequency hopping, direct sequence spreading, time scrambling, and combinations of these techniques are forms of spread spectrum.
spyware	Software that is secretly or surreptitiously installed into an information system to gather information on individuals or organizations without their knowledge; a type of malicious code.
start-up KEK (C.F.D.)	Key-encryption-key held in common by a group of potential communicating entities and used to establish ad hoc tactical networks.
steganography	The art, science, and practice of communicating in a way that hides the existence of the communication.
storage object (C.F.D.)	Object supporting both read and write accesses to an information system.
strength of mechanism (SoM)	A scale for measuring the relative strength of a security mechanism.
striped core	A network architecture in which user data traversing a core IP network is decrypted, filtered and re-encrypted one or more times.

Note: The decryption, filtering, and re-encryption are performed within a "Red gateway"; consequently, the core is "striped" because the data path is alternately Black, Red, and Black.

strong authentication	The requirement to use multiple factors for authentication and advanced technology, such as dynamic passwords or digital certificates, to verify an entity's identity.
subassembly (C.F.D.)	Major subdivision of an assembly consisting of a package of parts, elements, and circuits that perform a specific function.
subject	An active entity (generally an individual, process, or device) that causes information to flow among objects or changes the system state. See also object.
subject security level (C.F.D.)	Sensitivity label(s) of the objects to which the subject has both read and write access. Security level of a subject must always be dominated by the clearance level of the user associated with the subject.
Subordinate Certification Authority	In a hierarchal PKI, a Certification Authority whose certificate signature key is certified by another CA, and whose activities are constrained by that other CA.
subscriber	A party who receives a credential or token from a Credentials Service Provider (CSP) and becomes a claimant in an authentication protocol.
Suite A	A specific set of classified cryptographic algorithms used for the protection of some categories of restricted mission critical information.
Suite B	A specific set of cryptographic algorithms suitable for protecting both classified and unclassified national security systems and information throughout the US government and to support interoperability with allies and coalition partners.
superencryption	Process of encrypting encrypted information. Occurs when a message, encrypted off-line, is transmitted over a secured, on-line circuit, or when information encrypted by the originator is multiplexed onto a communications trunk, which is then bulk encrypted.
Superior Certification Authority	In a hierarchical PKI, a Certification Authority who has certified the certificate signature key of another CA, and who constrains the activities of that CA.
supersession	Scheduled or unscheduled replacement of COMSEC material with a different edition.
Supervisory Control and Data Acquisition System (SCADA)	Networks or systems generally used for industrial controls or to manage infrastructure such as pipelines and power systems.
supply chain	A system of organizations, people, activities, information, and resources, possibly international in scope, that provides products or services to consumers.

supply chain attack	Attacks that allow the adversary to utilize implants or other vulnerabilities inserted prior to installation in order to infiltrate data, or manipulate information technology hardware, software, operating systems, peripherals (information technology products) or services at any point during the life cycle.
suppression measure	Action, procedure, modification, or device that reduces the level of, or inhibits the generation of, compromising emanations in an information system.
surrogate access (C.F.D.)	See discretionary access control.
syllabary	List of individual letters, combination of letters, or syllables, with their equivalent code groups, used for spelling out words or proper names not present in the vocabulary of a code. A syllabary may also be a spelling table.
symmetric encryption algorithm	Encryption algorithms using the same secret key for encryption and decryption.
symmetric key	A cryptographic key that is used to perform both the cryptographic operation and its inverse, for example to encrypt and decrypt, or create a message authentication code and to verify the code.
synchronous crypto-operation	Method of on-line cryptographic operation in which cryptographic equipment and associated terminals have timing systems to keep them in step.
system	Any organized assembly of resources and procedures united and regulated by interaction or interdependence to accomplish a set of specific functions. See also information system.
System Administrator (SA)	Individual responsible for the installation and maintenance of an information system, providing effective information system utilization, adequate security parameters, and sound implementation of established Information Assurance policy and procedures.
system assets (C.F.D.)	Any software, hardware, data, administrative, physical, communications, or personnel resource within an information system.
System Development Life Cycle (SDLC)	The scope of activities associated with a system, encompassing the system's initiation, development and acquisition, implementation, operation and maintenance, and ultimately its disposal that instigates another system initiation.
system development methodologies (C.F.D.)	Methodologies developed through software engineering to manage the complexity of system development. Development methodologies include software engineering aids and high-level design analysis tools.
system high (C.F.D.)	Highest security level supported by an information system.

System High Mode	Information systems security mode of operation wherein each user, with direct or indirect access to the information system, its peripherals, remote terminals, or remote hosts, has all of the following: 1) valid security clearance for all information within an information system; 2) formal access approval and signed nondisclosure agreements for all the information stored and/or processed (including all compartments, sub compartments and/or special access programs); and 3) valid need-to- know for some of the information contained within the information system.
system indicator	Symbol or group of symbols in an off-line encrypted message identifying the specific cryptosystem or key used in the encryption.
system integrity	Attribute of an information system when it performs its intended function in an unimpaired manner, free from deliberate or inadvertent unauthorized manipulation of the system.
system interconnection	The direct connection of two or more information systems for the purpose of sharing data and other information resources.
system low (C.F.D.)	Lowest security level supported by an information system.
system owner	Person or organization having responsibility for the development, procurement, integration, modification, operation and maintenance, and/or final disposition of an information system.
system profile (C.F.D.)	Detailed security description of the physical structure, equipment component, location, relationships, and general operating environment of an information system.
system security (C.F.D.)	See information system security. Note: The relevant new term is Information Assurance.
System Security Plan (SSP)	The formal document prepared by the information system owner (or common security controls owner for inherited controls) that provides an overview of the security requirements for the system and describes the security controls in place or planned for meeting those requirements. The plan can also contain as supporting appendices or as references, other key security-related documents such as a risk assessment, privacy impact assessment, system interconnection agreements, contingency plan, security configurations, configuration management plan, and incident response plan.
systems security engineering	See Information Systems Security Engineering.
Systems Security Officer	See Information Systems Security Officer.
system-specific security control	A security control for an information system that has not been designated as a common control or the portion of a hybrid security control that is to be implemented within an information system.

T

tactical data	Information that requires protection from disclosure and modification for a limited duration as determined by the originator or information owner.
tactical edge	The platforms, sites, and personnel (U. S. military, allied, coalition partners, first responders) operating at lethal risk in a battle space or crisis environment characterized by 1) a dependence on information systems and connectivity for survival and mission success, 2) high threats to the operational readiness of both information systems and connectivity, and 3) users are fully engaged, highly stressed, and dependent on the availability, integrity, and transparency of their information systems.
tailoring	The process by which a security control baseline is modified based on 1) the application of scoping guidance, 2) the specification of compensating security controls, if needed, and 3) the specification of organization-defined parameters in the security controls via explicit assignment and selection statements.
tampering	An intentional event resulting in modification of a system, its intended behavior, or data.
Target Of Evaluation (TOE)	In accordance with Common Criteria, an information system, part of a system or product, and all associated documentation, that is the subject of a security evaluation.
Technical Reference Model (TRM)	A component-driven, technical framework that categorizes the standards and technologies to support and enable the delivery of service components and capabilities.
technical security controls	Security controls (i.e., safeguards or countermeasures) for an information system that are primarily implemented and executed by the information system through mechanisms contained in the hardware, software, or firmware components of the system.
technical vulnerability information	Detailed description of a weakness to include the implementable steps (such as code) necessary to exploit that weakness.
telecommunications	Preparation, transmission, communication, or related processing of information (writing, images, sounds, or other data) by electrical, electromagnetic, electromechanical, electro-optical, or electronic means.
TEMPEST	A name referring to the investigation, study, and control of compromising emanations from telecommunications and automated information systems equipment.
TEMPEST test (C.F.D.)	Laboratory or on-site test to determine the nature of compromising emanations associated with an information system.
TEMPEST zone	Designated area within a facility where equipment with appropriate TEMPEST characteristics (TEMPEST zone assignment) may be operated.
test key	Key intended for testing of COMSEC equipment or systems.

threat	Any circumstance or event with the potential to adversely impact organizational operations (including mission, functions, image, or reputation), organizational assets, individuals, other organizations, or the Nation through an information system via unauthorized access, destruction, disclosure, modification of information, and/or denial of service.
threat analysis	See threat assessment.
threat assessment	Process of formally evaluating the degree of threat to an information system or enterprise and describing the nature of the threat.
threat monitoring	Analysis, assessment, and review of audit trails and other information collected for the purpose of searching out system events that may constitute violations of system security.
threat source	The intent and method targeted at the intentional exploitation of a vulnerability or a situation and method that may accidentally exploit a vulnerability.
time bomb	Resident computer program that triggers an unauthorized act at a predefined time.
time-compliance date	Date by which a mandatory modification to a COMSEC end-item must be incorporated if the item is to remain approved for operational use.
time-dependent password	Password that is valid only at a certain time of day or during a specified interval of time.
TOE Security Functions (TSF) (C.F.D.)	Set consisting of all hardware, software, and firmware of the TOE that must be relied upon for the correct enforcement of the TOE Security Policy (TSP).
TOE Security Policy (TSP) (C.F.D.)	Set of rules that regulate how assets are managed, protected, and distributed within the TOE.
token	Something that the claimant possesses and controls (such as a key or password) that is used to authenticate a claim. See also cryptographic token.
Tradecraft Identity	An identity used for the purpose of work-related interactions that may or may not be synonymous with an individual's true identity.
Traditional INFOSEC program (C.F.D.)	Program in which NSA acts as the central procurement agency for the development and, in some cases, the production of INFOSEC items. This includes the Authorized Vendor Program. Modifications to the INFOSEC end-items used in products developed and/or produced under these programs must be approved by NSA.
Traffic Analysis (TA)	Gaining knowledge of information by inference from observable characteristics of a data flow, even if the information is not directly available (e.g., when the data is encrypted). These characteristics include the identities and locations of the source(s) and destination(s) of the flow, and the flow's presence, amount, frequency, and duration of occurrence.

Traffic Encryption Key (TEK)	Key used to encrypt plain text or to superencrypt previously encrypted text and/or to decrypt cipher text.
traffic padding	Generation of mock communications or data units to disguise the amount of real data units being sent.
Traffic-Flow Security (TFS)	Techniques to counter Traffic Analysis.
tranquility	Property whereby the security level of an object cannot change while the object is being processed by an information system.
transmission	The state that exists when information is being electronically sent from one location to one or more other locations.
transmission security (TRANSEC)	Measures (security controls) applied to transmissions in order to prevent interception, disruption of reception, communications deception, and/or derivation of intelligence by analysis of transmission characteristics such as signal parameters or message externals. Note: TRANSEC is that field of COMSEC which deals with the security of communication transmissions, rather than that of the information being communicated.
trap door	1. A means of reading cryptographically protected information by the use of private knowledge of weaknesses in the cryptographic algorithm used to protect the data. See also back door. 2. In cryptography, one-to-one function that is easy to compute in one direction, yet believed to be difficult to invert without special information.
triple DES (3DES)	An implementation of the Data Encryption Standard (DES) algorithm that uses three passes of the DES algorithm instead of one as used in ordinary DES applications. Triple DES provides much stronger encryption than ordinary DES but it is less secure than AES.
Trojan horse	A computer program that appears to have a useful function, but also has a hidden and potentially malicious function that evades security mechanisms, sometimes by exploiting legitimate authorizations of a system entity that invokes the program.
trust anchor	An established point of trust (usually based on the authority of some person, office, or organization) from which an entity begins the validation of an authorized process or authorized (signed) package. A "trust anchor" is sometimes defined as just a public key used for different purposes (e.g., validating a Certification Authority, validating a signed software package or key, validating the process (or person) loading the signed software or key).
trust list	The collection of trusted certificates used by relying parties to authenticate other certificates.

trusted agent (TA)	Entity authorized to act as a representative of an Agency in confirming subscriber identification during the registration process. Trusted agents do not have automated interfaces with Certification Authorities.
trusted certificate	A certificate that is trusted by the relying party on the basis of secure and authenticated delivery. The public keys included in trusted certificates are used to start certification paths. Also known as a "trust anchor."
trusted channel	A channel where the endpoints are known and data integrity is protected in transit. Depending on the communications protocol used, data privacy may be protected in transit. Examples include SSL, IPSEC, and secure physical connection.
trusted computer system	A system that employs sufficient hardware and software assurance measures to allow its use for processing simultaneously a range of sensitive or classified information.
Trusted Computing Base (TCB)	Totality of protection mechanisms within a computer system, including hardware, firmware, and software, the combination responsible for enforcing a security policy.
trusted distribution (C.F.D.)	Method for distributing trusted computing base (TCB) hardware, software, and firmware components that protects the TCB from modification during distribution.
trusted foundry	Facility that produces integrated circuits with a higher level of integrity assurance.
trusted identification forwarding (C.F.D.)	Identification method used in information system networks whereby the sending host can verify an authorized user on its system is attempting a connection to another host. The sending host transmits the required user authentication information to the receiving host.
trusted path	A mechanism by which a user (through an input device) can communicate directly with the security functions of the information system with the necessary confidence to support the system security policy. This mechanism can only be activated by the user or the security functions of the information system and cannot be imitated by untrusted software.
trusted process	Process that has been tested and verified to operate only as intended.
trusted recovery	Ability to ensure recovery without compromise after a system failure.
trusted software (C.F.D.)	Software portion of a trusted computing base (TCB).
trusted timestamp	A digitally signed assertion by a trusted authority that a specific digital object existed at a particular time.
trustworthiness	The attribute of a person or enterprise that provides confidence to others of the qualifications, capabilities, and reliability of that entity to perform specific tasks and fulfill assigned responsibilities.

TSEC nomenclature	System for identifying the type and purpose of certain items of COMSEC material.
tunneling	Technology enabling one network to send its data via another network's connections. Tunneling works by encapsulating a network protocol within packets carried by the second network.
two-part code (C.F.D.)	Code consisting of an encoding section, in which the vocabulary items (with their associated code groups) are arranged in alphabetical or other systematic order, and a decoding section, in which the code groups (with their associated meanings) are arranged in a separate alphabetical or numeric order.
Two-Person Control (TPC)	Continuous surveillance and control of positive control material at all times by a minimum of two authorized individuals, each capable of detecting incorrect and unauthorized procedures with respect to the task being performed and each familiar with established security and safety requirements.
Two-Person Integrity (TPI)	System of storage and handling designed to prohibit individual access by requiring the presence of at least two authorized individuals, each capable of detecting incorrect or unauthorized security procedures with respect to the task being performed. See no-lone zone.
Type 1 key (C.F.D.)	Generated and distributed under the auspices of NSA for use in a cryptographic device for the protection of classified and sensitive national security information.
Type 1 product (C.F.D.)	Cryptographic equipment, assembly or component classified or certified by NSA for encrypting and decrypting classified and sensitive national security information when appropriately keyed. Developed using established NSA business processes and containing NSA approved algorithms. Used to protect systems requiring the most stringent protection mechanisms.
Type 2 key (C.F.D.)	Generated and distributed under the auspices of NSA for use in a cryptographic device for the protection of unclassified national security information.
Type 2 product (C.F.D.)	Cryptographic equipment, assembly, or component certified by NSA for encrypting or decrypting sensitive national security information when appropriately keyed. Developed using established NSA business processes and containing NSA approved algorithms. Used to protect systems requiring protection mechanisms exceeding best commercial practices including systems used for the protection of unclassified national security information.
Type 3 key (C.F.D.)	Used in a cryptographic device for the protection of unclassified sensitive information, even if used in a Type 1 or Type 2 product.
Type 3 product (C.F.D.)	Unclassified cryptographic equipment, assembly, or component used, when appropriately keyed, for encrypting or decrypting unclassified sensitive U.S. Government or commercial information, and to protect systems requiring protection mechanisms consistent with standard commercial practices. Developed using established commercial standards and containing NIST approved cryptographic algorithms/modules or successfully evaluated by the National Information Assurance Partnership (NIAP).

Type 4 key (C.F.D.)	Used by a cryptographic device in support of its Type 4 functionality; i.e., any provision of key that lacks U.S. Government endorsement or oversight.
Type 4 product (C.F.D.)	Unevaluated commercial cryptographic equipment, assemblies, or components that neither NSA nor NIST certify for any Government usage. These products are typically delivered as part of commercial offerings and are commensurate with the vendor's commercial practices. These products may contain either vendor proprietary algorithms, algorithms registered by NIST, or algorithms registered by NIST and published in a FIPS.
type accreditation (*L)	A form of accreditation that is used to authorize multiple instances of a major application or general support system for operation at approved locations with the same type of computing environment. In situations where a major application or general support system is installed at multiple locations, a type accreditation will satisfy C&A requirements only if the application or system consists of a common set of tested and approved hardware, software, and firmware.
type certification (*L)	The certification acceptance of replica information systems based on the comprehensive evaluation of the technical and non-technical security features of an information system and other safeguards, made as part of and in support of the formal approval process, to establish the extent to which a particular design and implementation meet a specified set of security requirements.

U

U.S. person	Federal law and executive order define a U.S. Person as: a citizen of the United States; an alien lawfully admitted for permanent residence; an unincorporated association with a substantial number of members who are citizens of the U.S. or are aliens lawfully admitted for permanent residence; and/or a corporation that is incorporated in the U.S.
U.S.-controlled facility	Base or building to which access is physically controlled by U.S. individuals who are authorized U.S. Government or U.S. Government contractor employees.
U.S.-controlled space	Room or floor within a facility that is not a U.S.-controlled facility, access to which is physically controlled by U.S. individuals who are authorized U.S. Government or U.S. Government contractor employees. Keys or combinations to locks controlling entrance to U.S.-controlled spaces must be under the exclusive control of U.S. individuals who are U.S. Government or U.S. Government contractor employees.
unauthorized access	Any access that violates the stated security policy.
unauthorized disclosure	An event involving the exposure of information to entities not authorized access to the information.
unclassified	Information that has not been determined pursuant to E.O. 12958, as amended, or any predecessor order, to require protection against unauthorized disclosure and that is not designated as classified.

untrusted process	Process that has not been evaluated or examined for correctness and adherence to the security policy. It may include incorrect or malicious code that attempts to circumvent the security mechanisms.
update (certificate)	The act or process by which data items bound in an existing public key certificate, especially authorizations granted to the subject, are changed by issuing a new certificate.
update (key)	Automatic or manual cryptographic process that irreversibly modifies the state of a COMSEC key.
US-CERT	A partnership between the Department of Homeland Security and the public and private sectors, established to protect the nation's internet infrastructure. US-CERT coordinates defense against and responses to cyber attacks across the nation.
user	Individual, or (system) process acting on behalf of an individual, authorized to access an information system.
user ID	Unique symbol or character string used by an information system to identify a specific user.
User Partnership Program (UPP) (C.F.D.)	Partnership between the NSA and a U.S. Government agency to facilitate development of secure information system equipment incorporating NSA-approved cryptography. The result of this program is the authorization of the product or system to safeguard national security information in the user's specific application.
user representative (COMSEC)	Individual authorized by an organization to order COMSEC keying material and interface with the keying system, provide information to key users, and ensure the correct type of key is ordered.
user representative (Risk Management)	The person that defines the system's operational and functional requirements, and who is responsible for ensuring that user operational interests are met throughout the systems authorization process.

V

validation	Confirmation (through the provision of strong, sound, objective evidence) that requirements for a specific intended use or application have been fulfilled (e.g., a trustworthy credential has been presented, or data or information has been formatted in accordance with a defined set of rules, or a specific process has demonstrated that an entity under consideration meets, in all respects, its defined attributes or requirements).
variant	One of two or more code symbols having the same plain text equivalent.
verification	Confirmation, through the provision of objective evidence, that specified requirements have been fulfilled (e.g., an entity's requirements have been correctly defined, or an entity's attributes have been correctly presented; or a procedure or function performs as intended and leads to the expected outcome.

Virtual Private Network (VPN)	Protected information system link utilizing tunneling, security controls (see Information Assurance), and endpoint address translation giving the impression of a dedicated line.
virus	A computer program that can copy itself and infect a computer without permission or knowledge of the user. A virus might corrupt or delete data on a computer, use e-mail programs to spread itself to other computers, or even erase everything on a hard disk.
vulnerability	Weakness in an information system, system security procedures, internal controls, or implementation that could be exploited by a threat source.
vulnerability analysis	See vulnerability assessment.
vulnerability assessment	Systematic examination of an information system or product to determine the adequacy of security measures, identify security deficiencies, provide data from which to predict the effectiveness of proposed security measures, and confirm the adequacy of such measures after implementation.

W

warm site	Backup site which typically contains the data links and pre-configured equipment necessary to rapidly start operations, but does not contain live data. Thus commencing operations at a warm site will (at a minimum) require the restoration of current data.
web bug	Malicious code, invisible to a user, placed on web sites in such a way that it allows third parties to track use of web servers and collect information about the user, including IP address, host name, browser type and version, operating system name and version, and web browser cookie.
web risk assessment (C.F.D.)	Processes for ensuring websites are in compliance with applicable policies.
White Team	1. The group responsible for refereeing an engagement between a Red Team of mock attackers and a Blue Team of actual defenders of their enterprise's use of information systems. In an exercise, the White Team acts as the judges, enforces the rules of the exercise, observes the exercise, scores teams, resolves any problems that may arise, handles all requests for information or questions, and ensures that the competition runs fairly and does not cause operational problems for the defender's mission. The White Team helps to establish the rules of engagement, the metrics for assessing results and the procedures for providing operational security for the engagement. The White Team normally has responsibility for deriving lessons-learned, conducting the post engagement assessment, and promulgating results.

2. Can also refer to a small group of people who have prior knowledge of unannounced Red Team activities. The White Team acts as observers during the Red Team activity and ensures the scope of testing does not exceed a pre-defined threshold. |

Wi-Fi Protected Access-2 (WPA2)	The approved Wi-Fi Alliance interoperable implementation of the IEEE 802.11i security standard. For Federal government use, the implementation must use FIPS approved encryption, such as AES.
wiki	Web applications or similar tools that allow identifiable users to add content (as in an Internet forum) and allow anyone to edit that content collectively.
Wireless Access Point (WAP)	A device that acts as a conduit to connect wireless communication devices together to allow them to communicate and create a wireless network.
Wireless Application Protocol (WAP)	A standard that defines the way in which Internet communications and other advanced services are provided on wireless mobile devices.
wireless technology	Technology that permits the transfer of information between separated points without physical connection. Note: Currently wireless technologies use infrared, acoustic, radio frequency, and optical.
work factor	Estimate of the effort or time needed by a potential perpetrator, with specified expertise and resources, to overcome a protective measure.
Workcraft Identify	Synonymous with Tradecraft Identity.
worm	A self-replicating, self-propagating, self-contained program that uses networking mechanisms to spread itself. See malicious code.
write (C.F.D.)	Fundamental operation in an information system that results only in the flow of information from a subject to an object. See access type.
write access (C.F.D.)	Permission to write to an object in an information system.

X,Y

X.509 Public Key Certificate	The public key for a user (or device) and a name for the user (or device), together with some other information, rendered unforgeable by the digital signature of the certification authority that issued the certificate, encoded in the format defined in the ISO/ITU-T X.509 standard. Also known as X.509 Certificate.

Z

zero fill	To fill unused storage locations in an information system with the representation of the character denoting "0."
zeroization	A method of erasing electronically stored data, cryptographic keys, and Credentials Service Providers (CSPs) by altering or deleting the contents of the data storage to prevent recovery of the data.
zeroize	To remove or eliminate the key from a cryptographic equipment or fill device.

zone of control

Three dimensional space surrounding equipment that processes classified and/or sensitive information within which TEMPEST exploitation is not considered practical or where legal authority to identify and remove a potential TEMPEST exploitation exists.

REFERENCES

The following documents were used in whole or in part as background material in development of this policy:

a.   Public Law 107-347 [H.R. 2458], *The E-Government Act of 2002, Title III, the Federal Information Security Management Act of 2002*, December 2002.

b.   National Security Directive 42, *National Policy for the Security of National Security Telecommunications and Information Systems*, July 1990

c.   CNSSI No. 4016, *National Information Assurance Training Standard for Risk Analysts*, November 2005.

d.   Public Law 104-106, *Clinger-Cohen Act of 1996*, January 1996.

e.   Committee on National Security Systems Instruction (CNSSI) No. 4009, *National Information Assurance Glossary*.

f.   Public Law 108-458, *Intelligence Reform and Terrorism Act of 2004*, December 2004.

g.   Executive Order 13526, *Classified National Security Information,* December 29, 2009.

h.   Executive Order 13231, *Critical Infrastructure Protection in the Information Age,* October 2001.

i.   Executive Order 13388, *Further Strengthening the Sharing of Terrorism Information to Protect Americans*, October 2005.

j.   Office of Management and Budget Transmittal Memorandum No. 4, Circular A-130, *Management of Federal Information Resources*, November 2000.

k.   Department of Defense (DoD) Directive 8500.1, *Information Assurance,* October 2002.

l.   Director of Central Intelligence Directive 6/3, *Protecting Sensitive Compartmented Information Within Information Systems Manual,* June 1999.

m.   Federal Information Processing Standard Publication 200, *Minimum Security Requirements for Federal Information and Information Systems*, March 2006.

n.   Federal Information Processing Standard Publication 199, Standards for Security Categorization of Federal Information and Information Systems, February 2004

o.   National Security Telecommunications and Information Systems Security Directive No. 501, *National Security Program for Information Systems Security (INFOSEC) Professionals*, November 1992.

p.   CNSS Policy No. 6, *National Policy on Certification and Accreditation of National Security Systems*, October 2005.

q.   CNSS Directive No. 502, *National Directive on Security of National Security Systems*, December 2004.

r.   DoD Instruction 8500.2, *Information Assurance Implementation*, February 2003.

s.   CNSSI No. 4014, *Information Systems Security Officers National Information Assurance Training Standard*, March 2004.

t. National Institute of Standards and Technology (NIST) IR 7298, Glossary of Key Information Security Terms, April 2006

u. NIST SP 800-100, *Information Security Handbook: A Guide for Managers*, October 2006.

v. National Institute of Standards and Technology (NIST) Special Publication (SP) 800-30, *Risk Management,* July 2002.

w. NIST (SP) 800-53, Rev 3, *Recommended Security Controls for Federal Information Systems and Organizations*, Aug 09

x. Official (ISC)2® guide to the CISSP® CBK®: (ISC)2® Press / Harold F. Tipton, Kevin Henry

y. Intelligence Community Directive 503, *Information Technology Systems Security Risk Management, Certification and Accreditation*, 15 Sep 2008

z. Intelligence Community Policy Guidance No. 503.1, *Information and Information Systems Security Governance Roles and Responsibilities* (draft)

aa. NIST SP 800-37, *Guide for the Security Authorization of Federal Information Systems*, Rev 1, 2010

bb. CNSS Policy No. 22, *Risk Management Policy for National Security Systems*, March 2009

cc. RFC 4949, *Internet Security Glossary*, Version 2, August 2007

COMMONLY USED ABBREVIATIONS AND ACRONYMS

1.	ACL	Access Control List
2.	ADP	Automatic Data Processing
3.	AES	Advanced Encryption Standard
4.	AIG (C.F.D.)	Address Indicator Group
5.	AIN	Advanced Intelligence Network
6.	AK	Automatic Remote Rekeying
7.	AKP	Advanced Key Processor
8.	AKD/RCU	Automatic Key Distribution/Rekeying Control Unit
9.	ALC	Accounting Legend Code
10.	AMS	1. Auto-Manual System 2. Autonomous Message Switch
11.	ANDVT	Advanced Narrowband Digital Voice Terminal
12.	ANSI	American National Standards Institute
13.	APC	Adaptive Predictive Coding
14.	APU	Auxiliary Power Unit
15.	ASCII	American Standard Code for Information Interchange
16.	ASSIST Program	Automated Information Systems Security Incident Support Team Program
17.	AS&W	Attack Sensing and Warning
18.	ATC	Approval to Connect
19.	ATM	Asynchronous Transfer Mode
20.	ATO	Approval to Operate
21.	AUTODIN	Automatic Digital Network
22.	AVP	Authorized Vendor Program
23.	BoE	Body of Evidence
24.	BCP	Business Continuity Plan
25.	BIA	Business Impact Analysis
26.	BMA	Business Mission Area

27.	C2	Command and Control
28.	C3	Command, Control, and Communications
29.	C3I	Command, Control, Communications and Intelligence
30.	C4	Command, Control, Communications and Computers
31.	CA	1. Controlling Authority 2. Cryptanalysis 3. COMSEC Account 4. Command Authority 5. Certification Authority
32.	C&A	Certification and Accreditation
33.	CAC	Common Access Card
34.	CAW	Certificate Authority Workstation
35.	CC	Common Criteria
36.	CCB	Configuration Control Board
37.	CCEP	Commercial COMSEC Evaluation Program
38.	CCEVS	Common Criteria Evaluation and Validation Scheme
39.	CCI	Controlled Cryptographic Item
40.	CCO	Circuit Control Officer
41.	CD	Compact Disc
42.	CDS	Cross Domain Solution
43.	CEOI	Communications Electronics Operating Instruction
44.	CEPR	Compromising Emanation Performance Requirement
45.	CER	1. Cryptographic Equipment Room 2. Communication Equipment Room
46.	CERT	Computer (Security) Emergency Response Team
47.	CFD	Common Fill Device
48.	CIAC	Computer Incident Assessment Capability
49.	CIK	Cryptographic Ignition Key
50.	CIO	Chief Information Officer
51.	CIP	Critical Infrastructure Protection
52.	CIRC	1. Computer Incident Response Center 2. Computer Incident Response Capability
53.	CIRT	Computer Incident Response Team
54.	CISO	Chief Information Security Officer

55.	CKG	Cooperative Key Generation
56.	CKL	Compromised Key List
57.	CMCS	COMSEC Material Control System
58.	CNA	Computer Network Attack
59.	CND	Computer Network Defense
60.	CNE	Computer Network Exploitation
61.	CNO	Computer Network Operations
62.	CNSS	Committee on National Security Systems
63.	CNSSAM	Committee on National Security Systems Advisory Memorandum
64.	CNSSD	Committee on National Security Systems Directive
65.	CNSSI	Committee on National Security Systems Instruction
66.	CNSSP	Committee on National Security Systems Policy
67.	COG	Continuity of Government
68.	COI	Community of Interest
69.	COMPUSEC	Computer Security
70.	COMSEC	Communications Security
71.	CONOP	Concept of Operations
72.	COOP	Continuity of Operations Plan
73.	COR	1. Central Office of Record (COMSEC) 2. Contracting Officer Representative
74.	COTS	Commercial off-the-shelf
75.	CP	Certificate Policy
76.	CPS	Certification Practice Statement
77.	CPU	Central Processing Unit
78.	CRC	Cyclic Redundancy Check
79.	CRL	Certificate Revocation List
80.	Crypt/Crypto	Cryptographic-related
81.	CSA	Certificate Status Authority
82.	CSE	Communications Security Element
83.	CSIRT	Computer Security Incident Response Team
84.	CSN	Central Services Node
85.	CSP	Credentials Service Provider

86.	CSS	1. COMSEC Subordinate Switch
		2. Constant Surveillance Service (Courier)
		3. Continuous Signature Service (Courier)
		4. Coded Switch System
87.	CSSO	Contractor Special Security Officer
88.	CSTVRP	Computer Security Technical Vulnerability Report Program
89.	CTAK	Cipher Text Auto-Key
90.	CT&E	Certification Test and Evaluation
91.	CTTA	Certified TEMPEST Technical Authority
92.	CUI	Controlled Unclassified Information
93.	CUP	COMSEC Utility Program
94.	CVE	Common Vulnerabilities and Exposures
95.	DAA	1. Designated Accrediting Authority
		2. Delegated Accrediting Authority
		3. Designated Approval Authority
96.	DAC	Discretionary Access Control
97.	DAMA	Demand Assigned Multiple Access
98.	DAR	Data-at-Rest
99.	DCID	Director Central Intelligence Directive
100.	DCS	1. Defense Communications System
		2. Defense Courier Service
101.	DDoS	Distributed Denial of Service
102.	DDS	Dual Driver Service (courier)
103.	DEA	Data Encryption Algorithm
104.	DES	Data Encryption Standard
105.	DHCP	Dynamic Host Configuration Protocol
106.	DIACAP	DoD Information Assurance Certification and Accreditation Process
107.	DISN	Defense Information System Network
108.	DITSCAP	DoD Information Technology Security Certification and Accreditation Process
109.	DMA	Direct Memory Access
110.	DMS	Defense Message System
111.	DMZ	Demilitarized Zone

112.	DN	Distinguished Name
113.	DOC	Delivery-Only Client
114.	DoS	Denial of Service
115.	DRP	Disaster Recovery Plan
116.	DSA	Digital Signature Algorithm
117.	DSN	Defense Switched Network
118.	DSVT	Digital Subscriber Voice Terminal
119.	DTLS	Descriptive Top-Level Specification
120.	DTD	Data Transfer Device
121.	DTS	Diplomatic Telecommunications Service
122.	DUA	Directory User Agent
123.	EA	Enterprise Architecture
124.	EAL	Evaluation Assurance Level
125.	EAM	Emergency Action Message
126.	ECCM	Electronic Counter-Countermeasures
127.	ECM	Electronic Countermeasures
128.	ECPL	Endorsed Cryptographic Products List (a section in the Information Systems Security Products and Services Catalogue)
129.	ECU	End Cryptographic Unit
130.	EDAC	Error Detection and Correction
131.	EFD	Electronic Fill Device
132. (C.F.D.)	EFTO	Encrypt For Transmission Only
133.	EIEMA	Enterprise Information Environment Mission Area
134.	EKMS	Electronic Key Management System
135.	ELINT	Electronic Intelligence
136.	E Model	Engineering Development Model
137.	EMSEC	Emission Security
138.	EPL	Evaluated Products List (a section in the INFOSEC Products and Services Catalogue)
139.	EPROM	Erasable, Programmable, Read-Only Memory
140.	ERTZ	Equipment Radiation TEMPEST Zone

141.	ETPL	Endorsed TEMPEST Products List
142.	FAR	False Acceptance Rate
143.	FBCA	Federal Bridge Certification Authority
144.	FDIU	Fill Device Interface Unit
145.	FEA	Federal Enterprise Architecture
146.	FIPS	Federal Information Processing Standard
147.	FISMA	Federal Information Security Management Act
148.	FMR	False Match Rate
149.	FNMR	False Non-Match Rate
150.	FOCI	Foreign Owned, Controlled or Influenced
151.	FOUO	For Official Use Only
152.	FRR	False Rejection Rate
153.	FSRS	Functional Security Requirements Specification
154.	FSTS	Federal Secure Telephone Service
155.	FTS	Federal Telecommunications System
156.	FTAM	File Transfer Access Management
157.	FTLS	Formal Top-Level Specification
158.	GCCS	Global Command and Control System
159.	GETS	Government Emergency Telecommunications Service
160.	GIG	Global Information Grid
161.	GII	Global Information Infrastructure
162.	GOTS	Government-off-the-Shelf
163.	GPS	Global Positioning System
164.	GSS	General Support System
165.	GTS	Global Telecommunications Service
166.	GWEN	Ground Wave Emergency Network
167.	HAIPE	High Assurance Internet Protocol Encryptor
168.	HMAC	Hash- Based Message Authentication Code
169.	HSPD	Homeland Security Presidential Directive
170.	HTTP	Hypertext Transfer Protocol
171.	IA	Information Assurance
172.	I&A	Identification and Authentication

173.	IAB	Internet Architecture Board
174.	IAC	Information Assurance Component
175.	IAM	Information Assurance Manager
176.	IAO	Information Assurance Officer
177.	IATO	Interim Approval to Operate
178.	IATT	Interim Approval to Test
179.	IAVA	Information Assurance Vulnerability Alert
180.	IBAC	Identity Based Access Control
181.	IC	Intelligence Community
182.	ICANN	Internet Corporation for Assigned Names and Numbers
183.	ICVA	Intelligence Community Vulnerability Alert
184.	ICU	Interface Control Unit
185.	IDS	Intrusion Detection System
186.	IEMATS	Improved Emergency Message Automatic Transmission System
187.	IFF	Identification, Friend or Foe
188.	IFFN	Identification, Friend, Foe, or Neutral
189.	ILS	Integrated Logistics Support
190.	INFOSEC (C.F.D.)	Information Systems Security
191.	IO	Information Operations
192.	IP	Internet Protocol
193.	IPM	Interpersonal Messaging
194.	IPSec	IP Security
195.	IPSO	Internet Protocol Security Option
196.	IRM	Information Resources Management
197.	IS	Information System
198.	ISA	Interconnection Security Agreement
199.	ISDN	Integrated Services Digital Network
200.	ISE	Information Sharing Environment
201.	ISSE	Information Systems Security Engineer/Engineering
202.	ISSM	Information Systems Security Manager
203.	ISSO	Information Systems Security Officer
204.	IT	Information Technology

205.	ITAR	International Traffic in Arms Regulation
206.	ITSEC	Information Technology Security Evaluation Criteria
207.	IVA	Independent Validation Authority
208.	IV&V	Independent Verification and Validation
209.	KAK	Key-Auto-Key
210.	KDC	Key Distribution Center
211.	KEK	Key Encryption Key
212.	KG	Key Generator
213.	KMC	Key Management Center
214.	KMI	Key Management Infrastructure
215.	KMID	Key Management Identification Number
216.	KMODC	Key Management Ordering and Distribution Center
217.	KMP	1. Key Management Protocol
		2. Key Management Plan
218.	KMS	Key Management System
219.	KOA	KMI Operating Account
220.	KP	Key Processor
221.	KPC	KMI Protected Channel
222.	KPK (C.F.D.)	Key Production Key
223.	KSD	Key Storage Device
224.	LAN	Local Area Network
225.	LEAD	Low-Cost Encryption/Authentication Device
226.	LMD	Local Management Device
227.	LMD/KP	Local Management Device/Key Processor
228.	LOCK	Logical Co-Processing Kernel
229.	LPC	Linear Predictive Coding
230.	LPD	Low Probability of Detection
231.	LPI	Low Probability of Intercept
232.	LRA	Local Registration Authority
233.	LRIP	Low Rate Initial Production
234.	LSI	Large Scale Integration

235.	MAC	1. Mandatory Access Control 2. Message Authentication Code 3. Mission Assurance Category 4. Machine Addressable Code
236.	MAN	1. Mandatory Modification 2. Metropolitan Area Network
237.	MER	Minimum Essential Requirements
238.	MGC	Management Client
239.	MHS	Message Handling System
240.	MI	Message Indicator
241.	MIB	Management Information Base
242.	MIME	Multipurpose Internet Mail Extensions
243.	MINTERM	Miniature Terminal
244.	MISSI	Multilevel Information Systems Security Initiative
245.	MitM	Man-in-the-Middle Attack
246.	MLS	Multilevel Security
247.	MOU/A	Memorandum of Understanding/Agreement
248.	MSE	Mobile Subscriber Equipment
249.	MSL	Multiple Security Levels
250.	NACAM	National COMSEC Advisory Memorandum
251.	NACSI	National COMSEC Instruction
252.	NACSIM	National COMSEC Information Memorandum
253.	NAK	Negative Acknowledgement
254.	NCCD	Nuclear Command and Control Document
255.	NCS	1. National Communications System 2. National Cryptologic School 3. Net Control Station
256.	NCSC	National Computer Security Center
257.	NIAP	National Information Assurance Partnership
258.	NII	National Information Infrastructure
259.	NISAC	National Industrial Security Advisory Committee
260.	NIST	National Institute of Standards and Technology
261.	NLZ	No-Lone Zone

262.	NSA	National Security Agency
263.	NSD	National Security Directive
264.	NSDD	National Security Decision Directive
265.	NSEP	National Security Emergency Preparedness
266.	NSI	National Security Information
267.	NSS	National Security System
268.	NSTAC	National Security Telecommunications Advisory Committee
269.	NSTISSAM	National Security Telecommunications and Information Systems Security Advisory/Information Memorandum
270.	NSTISSC	National Security Telecommunications and Information Systems Security Committee
271.	NSTISSD	National Security Telecommunications and Information Systems Security Directive
272.	NSTISSI	National Security Telecommunications and Information Systems Security Instruction
273.	NSTISSP	National Security Telecommunications and Information Systems Security Policy
274.	NTCB	Network Trusted Computing Base
275.	NTIA	National Telecommunications and Information Administration
276.	NTISSAM	National Telecommunications and Information Systems Security Advisory/Information Memorandum
277.	NTISSD	National Telecommunications and Information Systems Security Directive
278.	NTISSI	National Telecommunications and Information Systems Security Instruction
279.	NTISSP	National Telecommunications and Information Systems Security Policy
280.	NVD	National Vulnerability Database
281.	OADR	Originating Agency's Determination Required
282.	OPCODE	Operations Code
283.	OPSEC	Operations Security
284.	ORA	Organizational Registration Authority
285.	OSI	Open Systems Interconnection Reference Model
286.	OTAD	Over-the-Air Key Distribution
287.	OTAR	Over-the-Air Rekeying
288.	OTAT	Over-the-Air Key Transfer

289.	OTP	One-Time Pad
290.	OTT	One-Time Tape
291.	PAA	(PKI) Policy Approving Authority (IC) Principal Accrediting Authority
292.	PAL	Permissive Action Link
293.	PBAC	Policy Based Access Control
294.	PBX	Private Branch Exchange
295.	PC	Personal Computer
296.	PCA	Policy Certification Authority
297.	PCIPB	President's Critical Infrastructure Protection Board
298.	PCMCIA	Personal Computer Memory Card International Association
299.	PDA	Personal Digital Assistant
300.	PDR	Preliminary Design Review
301.	PDS	1. Protected Distribution Systems 2. Practices Dangerous to Security
302.	PED	Portable Electronic Device
303.	PES	Positive Enable System
304.	PIA	Privacy Impact Assessment
305.	PII	Personally Identifiable Information
306.	PIN	Personal Identification Number
307.	PING	Packet Internet Groper
308.	PIV	Personal Identity Verification
309.	PKC	Public Key Cryptography
310.	PKE	Public Key Enabling
311.	PKI	Public Key Infrastructure
312.	PKSD	Programmable Key Storage Device
313.	P model	Preproduction Model
314.	PNEK	Post-Nuclear Event Key
315.	POA&M	Plan of Action and Milestones
316.	PPL	Preferred Products List (a section in the INFOSEC Products and Services Catalogue)
317.	PRBAC (C.F.D.)	Partition Rule Base Access Control
318.	PRM	Performance Reference Model

319.	PRNG	Pseudorandom Number Generator
320.	PROM	Programmable Read-Only Memory
321.	PROPIN	Proprietary Information
322.	PRSN	Primary Services Node
323.	PSN	Product Source Node
324.	PWDS	Protected Wire Distribution System
325.	RA	Registration Authority
326.	RAdAC	Risk Adaptable Access Control
327.	RAMP	Rating Maintenance Program
328.	RBAC	Role Based Access Control
329.	RMF	Risk Management Framework
330.	RNG	Random Number Generator
331.	ROM	Read-Only Memory
332.	RVTM	Requirements Verification Traceability Matrix
333.	SA	System Administrator
334.	SABI (C.F.D.)	Secret and Below Interoperability
335.	SAISO	Senior Agency Information Security Officer
336.	SAML	Security Assertion Markup Language
337.	SAO	Special Access Office
338.	SAP	1. System Acquisition Plan 2. Special Access Program
339.	SAPF	Special Access Program Facility
340.	SARK	SAVILLE Advanced Remote Keying
341.	SBU	Sensitive But Unclassified
342.	SCADA	Supervisory Control and Data Acquisition
343.	SCAP	Security Content Automation Protocol
344.	SCI	Sensitive Compartmented Information
345.	SCIF	Sensitive Compartmented Information Facility
346.	SDLC	System Development Life Cycle
347.	SDNS	Secure Data Network System
348.	SDR	System Design Review
349.	SFA	Security Fault Analysis

350.	SHA	Secure Hash Algorithm
351.	SFUG (C.F.D.)	Security Features Users Guide
352.	SI	Special Intelligence
353.	SISS	Subcommittee on Information Systems Security
354.	S/MIME	Secure/Multipurpose Internet Mail Extensions
355.	SMTP	Simple Mail Transfer Protocol
356.	SMU	Secure Mobile Unit
357.	SoM	Strength of Mechanism
358.	SPK	Single Point Key(ing)
359.	SRR	Security/System Requirements Review
360.	SRTM	Security Requirements Traceability Matrix
361.	SSAA	System Security Authorization Agreement
362.	SSL	Secure Socket Layer
363.	SSO	Staff Security Officer
364.	SSP	System Security Plan
365.	ST&E	Security Test and Evaluation
366.	STE	Secure Terminal Equipment
367.	STS	Subcommittee on Telecommunications Security
368.	STU	Secure Telephone Unit
369.	TA	1. Traffic Analysis
		2. Trusted Agent
370.	TACTERM	Tactical Terminal
371.	TAG	TEMPEST Advisory Group
372.	TCB	Trusted Computing Base
373.	TCP/IP	Transmission Control Protocol/Internet Protocol
374.	TED	Trunk Encryption Device
375.	TEK	Traffic Encryption Key
376.	TEP	TEMPEST Endorsement Program
377.	TFM	Trusted Facility Manual
378.	TFS	Traffic Flow Security
379.	TLS	Top-Level Specification
380.	TOE	Target of Evaluation

381.	TPC	Two-Person Control
382.	TPEP	Trusted Products Evaluation Program
383.	TPI	Two-Person Integrity
384.	TRANSEC	Transmission Security
385.	TRB	Technical Review Board
386.	TRI-TAC	Tri-Service Tactical Communications System
387.	TRM	Technical Reference Model
388.	TSABI (C.F.D.)	Top Secret and Below Interoperability
389.	TSCM	Technical Surveillance Countermeasures
390.	TSEC	Telecommunications Security
391.	TSF	TOE Security Functions
392.	TSP	TOE Security Policy
393.	TTAP	Trust Technology Assessment Program
394.	UA	User Agent
395.	UIS	User Interface System
396.	UPP	User Partnership Program
397.	USB	Universal Serial Bus
398.	VoIP	Voice over Internet Protocol
399.	VPN	Virtual Private Network
400.	WAN	Wide Area Network
401.	WAP	1. Wireless Access Point 2. Wireless Application Protocol
402.	WEP	Wired Equivalent Privacy
403.	WPA2	Wi-Fi Protected Access - 2
404.	XML	Extensible Markup Language